D0354280

Flawed Advice and the Management Trap

Recent Books by the Author

Flawed Advice and the Management Trap

*How Managers Can Know
When They're Getting Good
Advice and When They're Not*

CHRIS ARGYRIS

OXFORD
UNIVERSITY PRESS
2000

OXFORD
UNIVERSITY PRESS

Oxford   New York
Athens   Auckland   Bangkok   Bogotá   Buenos Aires
Calcutta   Cape Town   Chennai   Dar es Salaam   Delhi
Florence   Hong Kong   Istanbul   Karachi   Kuala Lumpur
Madrid   Melbourne   Mexico City   Mumbai   Nairobi   Paris
São Paulo   Singapore   Taipei   Tokyo   Toronto   Warsaw

and associated companies in
Berlin   Ibadan

Published by Oxford University Press, Inc.
198 Madison Avenue, New York, New York 10016

Oxford is a registered trademark of Oxford University Press, Inc.

Library of Congress Cataloging-in-Publication Data
Argyris, Chris, 1923–
Flawed advice and the management trap :
how managers can know when they're getting
good advice and when they're not / Chris Argyris.
p. cm.   Includes bibliographical references and index.
ISBN 0-19-513286-6
1. Business consultants.   2. Management.
3. Error.   I. Title.
HD69.C6A698   2000   658.4'012–dc21   99-32358

3 5 7 9 8 6 4

Printed in the United States of America
on acid-free paper

Contents

Preface

PEOPLE AND ORGANIZATIONS continually strive to achieve effective action. But they do not have to do so in isolation. Available to them, especially on non-routine issues of great importance, is a broad array of advice from executives, change consultants, and academics. This is especially true on topics having to do with organizational learning, transformational change, and employee commitment.

Much of this advice is appealing; much of it compelling. Providing it has become big business in its own right. The only problem is, most of it does not work—that is, most of it is not actionable. It is simply too full of abstract claims, inconsistencies, and logical gaps to be useful as a concrete basis for concrete actions in concrete settings.

How can this be? At base, it is my contention—and the core argument of this book—that this advice fails because it is based on an implicit theory of effective action that, by definition, is counterproductive when applied to important, non-routine issues. Those who provide it may honestly believe it to be true, relevant, and useful. But their belief is based on the very same theory of effective action that, when followed correctly, got them into trouble in the first place.

Again, how can this be? Their theory of action often makes advisors blind not only to the gaps and inconsistencies in their advice, but also to the fact that they are blind. What they say, therefore, is not the result of ignorance, but of skilled unawareness and skilled incompetence. Professionally, they are very good at being wrong. They are not alone.

Decades of research have shown that the vast majority of individuals—regardless of age, race, gender, education, wealth, or culture—adhere to the same theory of effective action. The organizations they build are, not surprisingly, based on it. The inevitable result: patterns of skilled unawareness and skilled incompetence that manifest themselves in complex defensive routines, which are themselves undiscussable. Worse, even their undiscussability is undiscussable.

This is not a question of odds or probabilities. Advice that derives from this theory cannot help leading to actions whose effectiveness is limited. Whatever the specific context of the advice—whether about programs for building transformational leaders, generating organizational learning, or developing internal commitment—the outcome will, at best, take the form of a short-lived fad. And the managers who rely on the advice will, at best, see their credibility undermined. Equally important, since none of this is discussable, colleagues will either distance themselves from taking constructive action or, if they do choose to face up to their organizations' defensive routines, will be met with cries of "immaturity," "foolishness," "romanticism," and "impracticability."

My goal in this book is to examine, in depth, why and how

most professional advice on non-routine issues continues to fail. The methodology I follow is to look with great care at a limited number of representative examples, which are drawn from my review of more than one hundred books and countless articles. I then place all this material in the context of a different theory of effective action—one that leads not to skilled incompetence, but to specific predictions that can be tested in real life.

Nearly two decades ago, I published a book that surveyed the action-oriented research in the academic literature (Argyris 1980). My judgment then, as now, was that most research on implementation was quite weak—not because the researchers' experience base was too limited or because their research designs were impractical. Now, as then, the problem lies with the implicit theory of action that underlies the questions they ask, the data they use, and the interpretations they make. I intend to show—in careful detail—exactly why that is so, as well as how a different theory of action can both illustrate these problems and correct them.

Cambridge, Massachusetts   C.A.
March 1999

Introduction

PRACTITIONERS AND SCHOLARS AGREE: twenty-first-century companies will be managed differently than twentieth century firms—especially in their approach to leadership, learning, and commitment. Getting there from here, or so the consensus runs, will require change that is transformational, discontinuous, non-routine, step-function, and creative. I agree. But with the advice commonly given on *how* to get there, I do not and cannot agree.

In my judgment, most of that advice is—most of the time—simply not actionable. And even if it is implemented correctly, it will lead to consequences that run counter to the intentions of those providing it.

Let me be clear. Those intentions are often fine, even enlightened. By any fair standard, however, much of the advice to which they give rise is full of gaps and inconsistencies. Now, advice does not come from nowhere but from some underlying framework and since thoughtful and well-intended advice givers do not intentionally offer counsel that is full of gaps and inconsistencies, there must be something in the frameworks on which they rely that makes them unaware of these problems—as well as unaware that they are unaware.

Model I

This should no longer be surprising. We have known for some time that the ideas about effective action in the frameworks people consciously use to design and craft non-routine and, possibly, embarrassing actions are not congruent with the nature and shape of the actions thus produced (Argyris 1982, 1990a, 1993; Argyris, Putnam, and Smith 1985; Argyris and Schön 1974, 1996). The reason, as we have discovered, is that we usually operate with two such frameworks—the one that we espouse and the one that we really employ.

As a rule, the first type of framework or design for action—the one we espouse—is something in which we believe so deeply that we are often willing to take risks to protect it. By contrast, the second is the one we actually use. It is what I call our "theory-in-use," and it is the key to how we act. Espoused theories often represent our ideas—indeed, our ideals—about effective action. Theories-in-use are what produce real, concrete actions.

Thus, there are inconsistencies between ideas about action and action itself. This has important consequences. When we are producing the actions, we are unaware of the gaps. But when others are producing the actions, *we are* aware of them—and of the fact that *they* are not. Patterned blindness occurs only when acting.

This matters because most theories-in-use are what my colleague, Donald Schön, and I have labeled "Model I." The governing values of Model I are :

- Be in unilateral control.
- Win; do not lose.
- Suppress negative feelings.
- Act as rationally as possible.

Shaped by these values, we tend to advocate our position, make evaluations of performance, and offer attributions about others' intentions in such a way that we remain in control, maximize our chances to win, and suppress negative feelings. In practice, this means that we act in ways that encourage neither inquiry into our views nor the robust testing of the claims that we make. Indeed, the only test possible under these conditions is one that uses self-referential logic: "Trust me, I know what I am doing."

As a result, Model I actions create defensiveness, self-fulfilling prophecies, self-sealing processes, and escalating error. All of these, in turn, reinforce the need for being in unilateral control, winning and not losing, suppressing negative feelings, and appearing rational. They also lead to Model I actors projecting blame for errors on others and on the system: "That's human nature," they say, or "Organizations always have these problems. That is the nature of the beast."

Why do people bypass their responsibilities in this way? Consistent with Model I, they are busy blaming others in ways that produce defensive dialogue, which, of course, they also blame on others. Equally important, they are unaware—and would heatedly deny assertions—that they are doing this. They are also very good at it. Indeed, their patterned blindness is the direct result of their being skilled at the behavior they are producing. If they were not, it would not be part of their theory-in-use.

Skillful behavior causes blindness because it

- Works.
- Appears to be effortless.
- Is taken for granted. (Indeed, the skillfulness can be lost if we pay conscious attention to it.)
- Appears spontaneous and automatic.

We are skillful when we no longer have to be aware of everything we learned that led to our being skillful. Thus, the prime evidence of acting skillfully is a kind of designed ignorance that I call "skilled unawareness." But since this type of skillful behavior regularly leads to counterproductive outcomes that are unmistakable signs of incompetence, it follows that Model I causes not only skilled unawareness but also skilled incompetence.

Model I—the master theory-in-use—exists in all industrialized cultures. It applies to everyone in those cultures—men and women, the rich and the poor, the well and the poorly educated, the young and the old. It is indifferent to religious, ethnic, and racial variations. It is as if Model I were wired into the human mind. Surface behavior may vary, but the underlying theory-in-use does not. It remains constant—and it scales.

Individuals programmed with Model I produce organizations that are consistent with Model I. Such organizations typically manifest defensive routines that are skillfully designed to prevent their members or constituent parts from experiencing embarrassment or threat. By definition, such routines are, as with individuals, overprotective and anti-learning.

Think, for example, of such common mixed messages as "John, be creative; but be careful" or "Mary, you are in charge, but check with William." There is an underlying logic at work here:

- State a message that is inconsistent.
- Act as if it is not inconsistent.
- Make all this undiscussable.
- Make the undiscussability undiscussable.
- Again, act as if you are not doing so.

Make no mistake: defensive routines—whether at the individual or the organizational level—are powerful. Efforts to "outlaw" them or to bypass them with new structures, new value statements, new policies, or new incentives do not work. Such efforts simply drive them underground, where they thrive. After all, Model I theories-in-use—like the advice to which they give rise—encourage and reward defensive routines.

Effective Advice

Action is effective to the extent that it leads to the consequences intended in ways that persevere—but without generating, as Model I does, unintended consequences that undermine the beneficial outcomes. Advice is effective to the extent that it is valid and actionable—that is, leads to effective action.

There are three tests for the validity of advice. If implemented correctly, it leads to the consequences that it predicts will occur; its effectiveness persists so long as no unforeseen conditions interfere; and it can be implemented and tested in the world of everyday practice.

There are four tests for the actionability of advice. It specifies the detailed, concrete behaviors required to achieve the intended consequences; it must be crafted in the form of designs that contain causal statements; people must have, or be able to be taught, the concepts and skills required to implement those causal statements; and the context in which it is to be implemented does not prevent its implementation.

In this book, I apply these criteria to representative examples of the advice in good currency about effective leadership, learning, change, and employee commitment, especially in situations that require non-trivial—that is, potentially enhancing or threatening—changes of the status quo. The books and articles chosen for review have sold thousands and, in some cases, millions of copies. They have been used in many companies and university programs. The advice they contain is measured and thoughtful—that is, it does not bypass controversial problems, nor does it deny that those problems are complex and cannot be fixed in minutes. The advice is also ambitious: its clear intent is to influence not only thinking about effective action, but also the action itself.

My critique of this material is based solely on the claims the various advice givers make and on the reasoning they use. I intentionally do not apply criteria of judgment external to those used by the advice givers, either explicitly or implicitly. For example, I do not critique their advice because it is not based on the normal requirements of scientific method. This is, in part, because I have already reviewed the relevant scholarly literature on the same topics (Argyris 1980, 1993; Argyris,

Putnam, and Smith 1985; Argyris and Schön, 1996). But it is also because any critique that is to lead to valid and actionable advice must be crafted with the use of reasoning that practitioners can reasonably be expected to apply in their everyday world.

For advice to be helpful, it must specify the intended outcomes or objectives to be produced, the sequence of actions required to produce them, the actions required to monitor and test for any errors or mismatches, and the actions required to correct such errors or mismatches. In other words, it must be crafted in terms of a theory-in-use about producing effective action. This is fine for routine matters, in which there is a fair level of consistency between espoused theory and theory-in-use. If two accountants begin with the same raw data, for example, they should come up with the same answers. If they do not, the agreed-on convention is to trace their steps backwards until the discrepancies are identified.

But it is not fine for non-routine situations, in which most theories-in-use are inadequate to produce the actions and outcomes they espoused. Advice so compromised is, in my terms, neither valid nor actionable. When the challenge is greatest and we need it most, far too much advice is often weakest and most misleading.

The Organization of the Book

In Chapters 1 and 2, I describe several representative examples of advice about effective leadership, learning, change, and employee commitment. I then apply a disciplined critique to these examples in order to surface their hidden, but important, gaps and inconsistencies. I do this to get at a more basic problem. These gaps and inconsistencies do not exist simply because of failed execution. They exist because of the theories-in-use with which we are all programmed early in life and the defensive routines to which they lead. The failures are the result of skilled incompetence.

How can I know that the authors selected do, indeed, have such theories-in-use? The answer does not lie in examining their espoused theories, but in making fine-grain analyses of their actual behavior as advice givers. These analyses follow the same explicit rules that have been used in thousands of cases to assess theories-in-use (Argyris 1982, 1990a, 1993; Argyris, Putnam, and Smith 1985).

Chapter 3 presents a theory of action that attempts to explain why these gaps and inconsistencies exist—and will continue to exist—as long as their basic causes are not corrected in such a way that the corrections persist. Chapter 4 describes the gaps and inconsitencies in current human resource practices.

Part II introduces the principles and examples that I will use to illustrate how effective corrective action can be taken. Such action does not come easily—much developmental effort is required. My key challenge here is to be as reflective as possible while producing advice and encouraging others to critique the advice I provide. There will, no doubt, be gaps and inconsistencies in what I say, but they should all be discussable.

Chapter 5 describes how readers can become more critical of the advice they read (including my own); Chapter 6 contains some new designs and approaches for appraising the performance of individuals and Chapter 7 has criteria for appraising group performance. Chapter 8 describes how to generate internal commitment to values, Chapter 9 explains how to generate internal commitment to implementing strategy, and Chapter 10 focuses on how to build generic competence in organizational learning. Chapter 11 contains the conclusion.

I should like to acknowledge the assistance of Alan Kantrow. He helped to frame the story in a way that was more focused, more readable, without losing its intended rigor. Nancy Nichols was very helpful in editing parts of the book. Steff Riordan worked hard to produce the manuscript. Finally, I acknowledge the assistance of Monitor Company in aiding me to conduct and implement the inquiry into this book.

PART I

Getting Flawed Advice

1

Inconsistent and Unactionable Advice

ONE OF THE MOST OFTEN-CITED BOOKS on personal leadership is Steven Covey's *Seven Habits of Highly Effective People* (1989), which is based on a set of principles that emphasize the importance of character and responsibility. Covey advises that the first step to effectiveness—a process that he calls "inside-out"—is to begin with one's self. From these basic principles, Covey derives such advice as: Develop trust, Generate positive energy, and Sidestep negative energy. The strategy is to be positive. The source of this positivism is a genuine caring for others, which depends, in turn, on first caring for one's self.

Covey provides a detailed example of how he used these principles in dealing with his son. But he makes it clear that the actions he took and the principles he followed apply to any situation where a "subordinate" is performing in a disappointing manner that does not meet jointly-arrived-at performance goals (pp. 175–179).

After a two-week discussion period, Covey decided to offer

his son the job of cleaning up the yard to "make it green and clean." Consistent with his philosophy, he wanted his son to own the responsibility for the task. To help assure his son's commitment, he made him the boss; he himself would be his son's helper. We pick up the conversation at this point:

I said. "You boss me."

"I do?"

"That's right. But my time to help is limited. Sometimes I'm away. But when I'm here, you tell me how I can help. I'll do anything you want me to do.

"Okay!"

"Now guess who judges you."

"Who?"

"You judge yourself."

"I do?"

"That's right. Twice a week the two of us will walk around the yard, and you can show me how it's coming. How are you going to judge?"

"Green and clean."

"Right!"

I trained him with those two words for two weeks before I felt he was ready to take the job. Finally, the big day came.

"Is it a deal, Son?"

"It's a deal."

"Green and clean."

"What's green?"

He looked at our yard, which was beginning to look better. Then he pointed next door. "That's the color of his yard."

"What's clean?"

"No messes."

"Who's the boss?"

"I am."

"Who's your helper?"

"You are, when you have the time."

"Who's the judge?"

"I am. We'll walk around two times a week and I can show you how it's coming."

"And what will we look for?"

"Green and clean."

Four days later, when the son had done nothing, Covey began to feel frustrated and somewhat betrayed. He describes his feelings as follows:

This was not acceptable. I was upset and disillusioned by his performance after two weeks of training and all those commitments. We had a lot of effort, pride, and money invested in the yard and I could see it going down the drain. Besides, my neighbor's yard was manicured and beautiful, and the situation was beginning to get embarrassing.

I was ready to go back to gofer delegation. Son, you get over here and pick up this garbage right now or else! I knew I could get the golden egg that way. But what about the goose? What would happen to his internal commitment?

So I faked a smile and yelled across the street, "Hi son. How's it going?"

"Fine!" he returned.

"How's the yard coming?" I knew the minute I said it I had broken our agreement. That's not the way we had set up an accounting. That's not what we had agreed.

So he felt justified in breaking it, too. "Fine, Dad."

I bit my tongue and waited until after dinner. Then I said, "Son, let's do as we agreed. Let's walk around the yard together and you can show me how it's going in your stewardship."

As we started out the door, his chin began to quiver. Tears welled up in his eyes and, by the time we got out to the middle of the yard, he was wimpering.

"It's so hard, Dad!"

What's so hard? I thought to myself. You haven't done a single thing! But I knew what was hard—self-management, self-supervision. So I said, "Is there anything I can do to help?"

"Would you, Dad?" he sniffed.

"What was our agreement?"

"You said you'd help me if you had time."

"I have time."

So he ran into the house and came back with two sacks. He handed me one. "Will you pick that stuff up?" He pointed to the garbage from Saturday night's barbecue. "It makes me sick!"

So I did. I did exactly what he asked me to do. And that was when he signed the agreement in his heart. It became his yard, his stewardship.

It is possible to generate a different set of lessons from this situation than those drawn in the text. Covey was, for example, enthusiastic about his son's accepting responsibility for taking care of the yard. He rehearsed and re-rehearsed with his son the basic features of the relationship. The son was responsible for judging his own performance, for being his own leader, and for using his father, when appropriate, as a helper. Covey was to act as a champion. The language used here should be familiar to those who read the literature on generating employee commitment.

Being a dedicated champion did not, however, work at the outset. The son did not respond as promised or as the champion expected. Again, this is a familiar situation in many commitment programs. Not surprisingly, Covey began to feel bewildered, upset, and betrayed. His automatic response was to take action that amounted to a reversal of the course he had been championing. Again, this is not news. Many champions have reported such feelings. But there *is* something newsworthy if we dig a bit further. Where did this reaction come from—given that it was clearly counterproductive to Covey's espoused theory of personal leadership?

Underneath this surface theory there exists an older, counterproductive routine that Covey activated in his mind, but was careful not to use. Why? Because he knew it was counterproductive, he suppressed it. Again, why? Because he felt it was important to be positive. And what is positive about suppressing bewilderment? Bewilderment, after all, was not, by itself, likely to make the son defensive, nor was it likely to make it easy for the son to accuse his father of acting in ways that violated their mutual promise.

Now, step back a moment and look at this from a different angle. What Covey actually does is suppress his feelings—and, even more important, he covers up the fact that he is doing so. The issue here is that, although Covey advises people to act authentically, he himself does not do so. Suppression and cover-ups do not lead to authenticity. Patience that translates into several days of false behavior and smiling even though the smile is fake simply do not create authenticity—even if done in the name of being positive and caring. Genuine trust and caring cannot be produced by inauthentic actions. Nor by the pretense that what is going on is not inauthentic.

The advice is clear. If trust were really being developed, what prevented the son, during the first day, from saying, "Dad, I am unable to fulfill my commitment because some of the garbage makes me feel sick"? If he had, I believe that Covey would have been delighted to pitch in and help. The fact is that, in practice, the son had not really accepted that, as a "subordinate," he could ask his dad to help him. True, his father had championed this possibility. And true, the son had promised he would do so. But neither was enough. By themselves, rehearsal and agreement were inadequate.

Subordinates are often embarrassed to admit they are hesitant to take initiatives that they have been invited—and have agreed—to take. This puts them in a double bind. If they hide their feelings, they are violating the relationship. But if they expose them, they will be admitting that they are bypassing their earlier agreement and acting as if they were not doing so.

Moreover, if they are aware that they are not performing as promised and that their supervisors feel frustrated and upset, how can they express these feelings without violating a theory of personal leadership that advises them to be positive? Perhaps by covering up and keeping silent they are, in their own view, being positive?

A further complication, of course, is that, in the name of positiveness and patience, the necessary work is not getting done. What if this happened in an organizational setting in which others were privy to the promises of performance? Might they not begin to wonder what the boss was waiting for? But, if they followed Covey's advice, they might see these questions as generating negative energy and defensiveness. So they would suppress them and then act as if they were not doing so.

We can now see that, embedded in Covey's theory of personal leadership, as illustrated in this example, is a causal scenario that goes something like this:

1. Create trust because that is the highest form of human motivation.
2. If you create trust, you will bring out the best in people.
3. Be patient.
4. If you follow the advice, everyone involved will benefit and, ultimately, much more work will get done in much less time.

If we examine this scenario closely, we find that it has some troublesome features. The causal claims are crafted in ways that cannot be tested in real life. The theory does not, for example, tell potential leaders how to create trust without also producing mistrust. Nor is it clear how a combination of trust and mistrust, accompanied by cover-ups, will bring out the best in people. Nor is it possible to know when patience is a defense.

Even so, Covey writes, "I am convinced that both partners will benefit [if they follow my advice]." Although I honestly doubt this claim, it may well be true. My problem is not that Covey makes this claim. It is that he makes it in ways that cannot be tested by a potential user. Let me be clear. The theory is morally attractive. Personally, I like the emphasis given such qualities as personal responsibility, authenticity, trust, genuine caring, and self-acceptance. I just cannot see how these qualities get produced by implementing his theory.

If my analysis is correct so far, there is another important problem. Covey would certainly not write a book that he know to contain the gaps and inconsistencies that I have illustrated. That means he must be unaware of those gaps and inconsistencies—and unaware that he is unaware. How do we explain this unawareness?

First, as noted above, the structure of his framework does not include provisions for questioning or testing it. More troublingly, as I hope to show in Chapter 3, like most people, Covey employs two mutually inconsistent theories of effective action: the one that he espouses and the one that he actually uses.

Developing Effective Groups and Meetings

Doyle and Strauss (1982) are consultants who help management groups produce effective meetings. They have developed a strong practice with some of the largest and most sophisticated organizations in the United States and elsewhere. Part of their advice focuses on routines that are likely to help make meetings work. This advice is straightforward. But there is another part of their advice, which deals with how to handle difficult issues of group performance. This I find problematic.

According to Doyle and Strauss, if a group is having difficulty in deciding where it wants to begin and how, the best thing to do is wait until it is convinced it needs you. Then, when it asks you to take more control, take it and give direction as to the actions required.

Reasonable? Certainly. But what are the cues that would

lead an advisor or leader to become convinced that a group needs help? Is it long silences? Is it discussions that go in circles and get nowhere? Should an advisor tell a group that he or she is waiting for the right cues? Or what the "right" cues are?

Doing so might, of course, lead to a self-fulfilling prophecy, in which group members intentionally produce the awaited cues so that they can get the advisor to take charge. If this happens, group members will likely not be candid about their strategy and so will tend to learn that covering up is part of effective group functioning. But if the advisor says nothing, does not this withholding of important information also require a cover-up? And how does that help develop the trust so crucial to the authors' advice? Indeed, even if a group found such intervention helpful, if the explanation of delay until a specific request for help was made was that "I wanted to encourage you to be in charge," could not someone legitimately ask why that had not been made explicit?

Or consider the problem of a group that is hung up or fixated. The authors' advice is to slow the group down: "We have plenty of time left. Let's make sure we're all together." The assumption underlying this type of proposed intervention is that a group that is stalled can undo its defensive reactions by slowing down. But how does slowing down lead to more effective action? If group members, acting naturally and at normal speed, produce group hang-ups, how does slowing down help them get together since they have not been able to do so up until now? Here, again, the issue is not surface reasonableness, but unexplained—and unexplored—gaps and inconsistencies in the advice given, as well as the absence of any sanctioned approach to test those recommendations.

Suppose, further, that an advisor believes a group is manip- ulating him or her to make choices for them. The authors' advice: wait them out, perhaps saying, "I need some help. What do you think that we should do next?" In other words, cover up the inference that the group is being manipulative.

Now, in order to implement such a cover-up, an advisor, we are told, must cover up the cover-up—in this case, by asking for help. But why? Is this not important information for group members to have? How can we know when to tell them and when not?

Or take yet another example: some movement is needed, and group members are either unaware of it or do not pro- duce it. The authors' counsel: take the proverbial bull by the horns and say, "Well, since there don't seem to be any strong feelings, one way or the other, I suggest we try . . . ."

As Chapter 3 shows in more detail, a group's actions that produce no movement are themselves skillful, as is its individ- ual, as well as collective, unawareness. Thus, the problem identified by the authors is produced skillfully—that is, not by accident but by the designs the members have in their heads. Similarly, errors of this type are generated by skill, not by holes in the members' heads.

As a result, the advice bypasses the responsibility the mem- bers have for skillful behavior that results in counterproduc- tive outcomes. "Taking the bull by the horns" is, here, a way to bypass the underlying problem. If the actions taken turn out to be helpful, the group will evaluate the leader positively, which is likely to reinforce their dependence on him or her. And this, in turn, will actually help the group keep the leader away from the underlying causes while acting as if this were not the case.

The illustrations vary, but the theme is constant: Doyle and Strauss consistently recommend strategies that would have a leader deal with difficult, potentially embarrassing issues by taking charge and guiding the group through troubled waters. Advice of this kind, though appealing, does not specify the actual behaviors that will help a leader effectively take charge. "Wait until they are convinced," "Slow down the group," and "Wait them out" do not stipulate precisely which actions constitute effective waiting or slowing down. Nor do they set out the criteria to be used to check whether the actions taken are valid and not superficial, or whether they are taken too early or too late.

A related problem is that most of this advice on taking charge is accompanied by an injunction for the leader to act as if he or she were not doing so. The mechanism at work here is bypass and cover-up. Because this mechanism is consistent with the defenses that exist in most groups, such advice may lead to a more efficient meeting, especially where the issues at stake are routine and straightforward, not embarrassing or threatening.

If so, however, the efficiency is created entirely by the skill of the leader, which makes the group more dependent, not more competent, in dealing with difficult issues in the future. In fact, it may encourage them to focus on routine, straightforward issues at the expense of more difficult ones or even to reinterpret non-routine issues as being routine ones. And it may encourage others to collude in keeping them blind to what they are really doing—all in the name of caring, providing support, and being civilized.

I do not believe that the authors are unaware that such consequences can occur. Nor do I believe that they are deliberately trying to design such consequences. What I do believe is that they are unaware of the extent to which following their advice creates and reinforces these consequences.

Real Change Leaders

Real Change Leaders, by Jon Katzenback, et al. (1995) is a book that describes managers who have been successful at bringing about organizational change that is revolutionary, that questions and uproots established practices. These Real Change Leaders (RCLs) exhibit limitless energy for hard work, as well as a commitment to meeting challenges and producing high performance. RCLs also continually challenge the status quo. They enjoy changing what appears to be unchangeable and making discussable what has been undiscussable. They are dedicated to learning in the service of change.

The authors make it clear that RCLs exhibit a great deal of care and concern for other people. They are committed to genuine democratic participation and are good at capturing the creative energy in every individual. They do so by being open, honest, and asking everyone, including themselves, to be dedicated to facing reality.

Two things about this argument are troubling. First, RCLs are said to empower everyone by requiring results and accountability, yet their own words strongly suggest this is not so. And, second, RCLs are said to be both tough and participative. Again, their own statements do not illustrate this claim.

One RCL, Mary, describes her actions as follows:

> I brought them in, and just started talking—for about an hour and a half—about all the things that I had been thinking about.

We all began to realize that the potential of this was phenomenal if we could just pull it together. All I can tell you is that when they came back with their final work, it knocked my socks off (p. 95).

Embedded in Mary's brief description are several claims (summarized in the left-hand column), about which I raise a series of questions (in the right).

CLAIMS	QUESTIONS
1. I talked for an hour-and-a-half.	1. What did she say? How did she craft it? If RCLs are concerned about employees taking initiative and empowering themselves, how does an hour-and-a-half broadcast cause that?
2. It caused everyone to realize the potential if they pulled it together.	2. What did Mary and others say that caused the realization? What does "pulling it together" mean? How was it caused?
3. It caused final products that were excellent.	3. What actually caused these products? Was it Mary? Was it the way Mary dealt with her people? What contributions did her people make?

Mary is saying, in effect, I know what happened; the inferences that I made are valid; and my conclusions are correct. In other words, Mary crafts her claim as, "Trust me, I am right." This is the equivalent of telling others that, if they think the way she does, then they will see the light. Her logic—and that of most of the RCLs cited—is self-referential. If it works, it does not work for the reasons given by the RCLs, but because of the coercion that they place on others to follow them.

Why did the authors not ask the kinds of questions I pose above? The answers to such questions are exactly what others need if they are to implement Mary's claims. How can someone be successful like Mary without knowing precisely what she said, what the employees said, and how she responded. How did Mary cause people to pull together? How did she know that what she did and said could be productive? Or that, in fact, it was? Perhaps there were other causes for their behavior, such as a realization that their jobs and their firm were in jeopardy.

George, another RCL, devised a strategy to cut the costs of making Compaq computers, yet he was unable to convince his superiors in Houston to approve the plan. So he just went ahead and took the risk himself. George and his colleagues described the days that followed as full of tough actions and plenty of blood, sweat, and tears. But what does all this mean in terms of actual behavior? Again, what we get is a black box.

Clearly, George did have courage. But what does his example teach us about how to produce such courage? What did George say, and what did he choose not to say? How did he craft the former and cover up the latter? What was the reasoning behind these choices? What were the defensive reactions of top management? How did George respond to them? We don't know.

Further, how did George communicate with his own people that he was going to bypass the top? What did he say, if anything, about how he was going to cover up the bypass? What was George teaching his subordinates about the defenses of those at the top? And how did these subordinates communicate to their subordinates? George may have helped get something important done in ways that unwittingly reinforced the defensive routines of the organization that so frustrated him in the first place. Again, we don't know.

At the same time, the more we look into the details we are given, the more we realize the gaps between the authors' description of what the RCLs did and what the RCLs say they did. For all the talk about "genuine participation," "democratic principles," "joint accountability," and "open dialogue," the RCLs consistently describe themselves as acting unilaterally.

Transforming Organizations

Kotter (1996) identifies eight errors that regularly lead to failure in efforts to transform organizations. The are: (1) allowing too much complacency, (2) failing to create a sufficiently powerful guiding coalition, (3) underestimating the power of vision, (4) undercommunicating the vision, (5) permitting obstacles to block the vision, (6) failing to create short-term wins, (7) declaring victory too soon, and (8) neglecting to anchor changes firmly in the corporate culture. These errors are, Kotter argues, often the reason that new strategies are not implemented well, acquisitions do not achieve expected synergies, reengineering takes too long and costs too much, downsizing does not get costs under control, and quality programs do not deliver hoped-for results. Kotter claims, I think correctly, that these errors exist throughout most organizations and that they persist over time.

Errors are mismatches between intention and what actually happens. Errors result from ignorance or unawareness. By definition, it is not possible to create them on purpose because, if you implement what you design, that is a match, not a mismatch. The mismatches Kotter cites are embedded in important words and phrases: *allowing too much* complacency, *failing* to create, *underestimating*, *undercommunicating*, and *neglecting*.

Why do managers produce such errors time and again? It cannot be, as many claim, that they have no choice because the defensive routines of their organizations coerce them into behaving in ways that sidestep real problems. The reason is simple. If they were coerced, then the errors produced are not mismatches, but matches that happen to be consistent with defensive routines of the sort illustrated by Kotter in his discussions of inwardly focused culture, paralyzing bureaucracy, parochial politics, low levels of trust, and arrogant attitudes reinforced by the status quo.

Here, for example, is how Kotter suggests that managers repair what he sees to be a common mismatch-based error: failed efforts to create a high sense of urgency among employees. The approach: observe those who have faced such problems in the past. Consider, say, Adrian, the head of a division in a large company, who realized that few others in his organization saw the dangers and opportunities facing the division. Consistent with Model I theory-in-use, he believed that the problem was not insurmountable and that managers who resisted could be "induced, pushed, or replaced."

Adrian was, of course, making attributions to—and evaluations of—his colleagues. He did not, however, test their validity with those involved. If he had, he may have discovered that they were indeed blind and so could have developed actions to help them reduce their blindness. Or he could have discovered that they were not blind. In which case, they could have found out that their complacency was produced because they adhered to organizational defensive routines. Or he could have discovered that his colleagues were not complacent, but had been acculturated to be passive and not take initiative.

Adrian's colleagues were also skilled at Model I theories-in-use. They could be blind to their own limitations and blind to the fact that they were blind. In addition, they could deal with these embarrassing and threatening issues by bypassing their feelings and covering up the bypass. Given such bypass and cover-up, they would not be likely to level with their superiors publicly—or with each other.

Under conditions like these, it makes sense to conclude, as Kotter does, that the Adrians of the world overestimate how much they can force changes and underestimate how hard it is to drive people out of their comfort zones. It also makes sense to conclude that the Adrians of the world may be blind to how their actions might inadvertently reinforce the status quo. Trying to establish a sense of urgency may, therefore, be incorrect advice. It may be, for example, that the players already do feel bewildered about how to act, which leads to a sense of urgency that supports organizational defensive routines. No mismatch here. Causes lead to predictable effects—even if those effects happen to be counterproductive.

In other words, Kotter's advice—raise the urgency level by creating a crisis, eliminating perks, setting stretch performance goals, using broader measures of performance, and insisting that people talk more frequently to disgruntled customers, suppliers, and shareholders—could both raise the level of urgency *and* make it easier for complacent employees not to examine their complacency. Eliminating perks, for example, could send a signal that is cosmetic and fails to engage the causes of complacency. Setting stretch goals could enhance performance and bypass the question of why employees were not doing so in the first place. Even if the advice has positive consequences, its very success may also produce counterproductive outcomes that strengthen complacency and drive it underground.

Executive Insight

The fundamental assumption behind the kind of advice under discussion is that it is valid and actionable. The advisors promise—and most users appear to accept the promise—that, if the advice gets implemented correctly, the promised consequences will follow. The causal claim is straightforward. It is also doubtful.

This is not because some actions controlled by the users might get in the way. Instead, it is, as we have seen, a direct result of the gaps and inconsistencies built into the framework from which the advice is derived. But it is also a result of the theories-in-use that are likely to be triggered when the advice is implemented. These theories will produce results that are counterproductive, generate a systematic unawareness of this counterproductiveness, and activate defensive routines that reinforce both the results and the unawareness of them. The cycle is vicious, and it is closed.

This is true even when the advice comes not from external

experts but from leading managers themselves. Consider, for example, these observations by Henry B. Schacht, formerly CEO of Cummins Engine (Horton, 1986, p. 286):

STATES	LEAVES UNSPECIFIED
"I know only that we had good people and a discipline to approach the situation, plus a high degree of good humor and a good sense of our own fallibility."	What are the characteristics of "good people"? What are the features of a "good disciplined approach" and a "good sense of our own fallibility"? How would one recognize them?
"We work very hard at a sense of collective responsibility and collective performance."	How to produce collective responsibility and collective performance under conditions of embarrassment or threat.
"But that doesn't mean there isn't individual responsibility within that. (One) must blend the individual within a general sense of sharing."	How to produce the blend, especially when the forces are against it.

and by James Burke, formerly CEO of Johnson and Johnson (Horton, 1986, p. 15):

STATES	LEAVES UNSPECIFIED
"It's only natural for people to want to tell me how things are going at the moment, but I tell them to talk about the future."	How does he divert them from the natural to doing something less natural? Why is it less natural in the first place?
"I don't think it bruises people to argue and debate. You'd be surprised how easy some of our young people find it to politely say, 'you know, you're wrong . . . you don't have the facts . . . I do, and here's the evidence to prove it.'"	How do they react to him? Are they upset? Do they cover-up? Does it make any difference to Burke? If so, how does he deal with it?
	How do they talk politely, and not bruise, when they talk about other people's defensive routines and fancy footwork?
	How do they encourage confrontation of their own views if this is what they say? What is the impact on the problem-solving process if there are individuals who find this model approach counterproductive?

and by Frank T. Cary, formerly CEO of IBM (Horton, 1986, p. 186):

STATES	LEAVES UNSPECIFIED
"I learned the technique of intense questioning. When someone came and started to make a presentation, I would stop them at the outset." (p. 202)	How does he produce intense questioning without making people intense? If it is all right for them to become intense, how does he deal with these feelings? How does he recognize them if they choose to cover up? How would he stop them? What would he say?
"I'd ask, 'What is it that you're recommending?' I made them explain in a way that was meaningful." (p. 202)	
	How does he recognize a meaningful way from a non-meaningful way? How does he act to make them explain in a meaningful way?
"All IBM managers are motivated to do a job; one of IBM's great strengths. The trick is a matter of knowing how to set the agenda . . . to get people working together." (p. 203)	Why do executives explain issues in nonmeaningful ways in the first place? Are they unaware of doing so? If so, why?
	What does he actually say, and how does he act to set the agenda to get people

"When he was in charge of corporate staff he encouraged them to operate in a contention mode. When he became general manager of the data processing group, he changed his agenda to eliminating contention and conflict." (p. 203)

working together? Why do they need someone to set the agenda if they are motivated to do a good job? Why don't they set the agenda the way he would?

What did he say and do to encourage contention?

What did he say and do to discourage contention? Any ideas of why he needed to do this in the first place?

The advice these executives give is abstract. It does not tell the reader what behavior is required to implement it. If people talk about the present, get them to talk about the future. If they make presentations in nonmeaningful ways, press them to make meaningful ones. If they lack a disciplined approach, get them to be more disciplined. Such talk is neither helpful nor actionable.

Nor do these advice givers make distinctions between errors that are due to ignorance and those that are designed. It is one thing if they simply do not know how to do what they urge others to do. It is quite another if, as is more likely, the errors are designed. In that case, what's missing is counsel on how to separate undesigned from designed error, as well as on how to find out what causes executives to produce designed errors in the first place and then to cover them up.

Without such clarity, much executive-generated advice reinforces the defensive patterns of their organizations. Reginald Jones of General Electric periodically sought honest feedback from his immediate subordinates. His practice was to assign an executive whom everyone trusted to chair key meetings. He did so because he assumed that individual and organizational defensive routines were so strong that subordinates could not level directly with their superiors, especially when the issues at stake were embarrassing or threatening.

Note, however, that Jones never tested the validity of his assumptions with his subordinates. Instead, he covered up his attribution and acted as if he were not covering up. No matter how good his motives, strategies like his are likely to make present problems self-fulfilling and the counterproductive reasoning underlying them self-sealing.

All these examples of professional advice have much in them of real merit. But a close examination reveals a pattern of gaps and inconsistencies that get very much in the way of the positive outcomes each author so clearly desires. We need to better understand the costs—often the hidden costs—of this pattern, as well as the unintended consequences to which it so often leads.

2

Organizational Consequences of Using Inconsistent Advice

CHAPTER 1 ILLUSTRATED how even the most highly-regarded advice about producing effective leadership, learning, and internal commitment contains important gaps and inconsistencies. Nevertheless, the advice is widely used. This often leads to counterproductive outcomes.

Consider, for example, the policies and practices intended to produce organizations that are global, competitive, flexible, and innovative. Underlying these policies and practices is a near unanimous agreement about the importance of people. As one CEO said, "No vision, no strategy can be achieved without able and dedicated employees." And top executives are clear about what they want from such employees:

- An unwavering interest in the best interests of the corporation
- A dedication to winning competitive battles and beating the competition
- Breakthrough performance

38

- Continual improvement
- Commitment to learning

Bauman, Jackson, and Laurence (1997), in an engrossing discussion of organizational change, say that the future of corporations is based on employees who have an enduring desire to be challenged and to win, as well as a commitment to continuous improvement and to learning of all kinds—especially those that keep an organization competitive, alert, flexible, and effective.

Jack Welsh, CEO of General Electric, spearheaded a program on employee commitment and ownership. He said that he wanted workers on the factory floor to be obsessed with the business and to feel like they owned their equipment. He also wanted them to apply continual pressure on their bosses and their peers for high performance.

Today, these are fairly common sentiments among top-level managers. In this chapter, I want to dig deeper into them. Beneath the rhetoric, there often lurk inner contradictions that, although rarely acknowledged, have profound implications. Indeed, in my experience, many of the best-intentioned claims about how to be more effective, if carried out correctly, lead to less effectiveness. They are, implicitly, designed that way.

Just think, for a moment, about the most common advice in good currency on designing and implementing programs for organizational improvement and change:

1. Define a vision.
2. Define a competitive strategy that is consistent with the vision.

3. Define organizational work processes that, when carried out, will implement the strategy.
4. Define individual job requirements so that employees can produce the processes effectively.

The advice makes sense. It is, indeed, rational to start with a clear, comprehensive, general framework and to work downward to steps that are increasingly concrete and local. No inner contradictions here. They appear when someone tries to implement the advice—build commitment, for example—in real life.

Much of the current advice about building commitment ignores the fact that it comes in two very different types. Both are valuable. Both can lead to persistence, endurance, and vigilance. Both can coexist. But the consequences to which each leads are naturally contradictory.

Commitment can be external or internal. These differ in how they are activated and in the source of energy they utilize. External commitment is triggered by management policies and practices that enable employees to accomplish their tasks. Internal commitment derives from energies internal to human beings that are activated because getting a job done is intrinsically rewarding.

When managers ask for commitment, they usually want employees to:

- Implement the strategy, process, and job requirements as faithfully, reliably, and effectively as they can.
- Monitor such implementation to assess effectiveness.
- Be vigilant about recognizing actual or potential gaps, errors, and inconsistencies, as well as new and unrecognized challenges.

The first two points can be implemented by the use of either external or internal commitment. The third requires internal commitment because it asks employees to go beyond what is defined by vision, strategy, and management process—indeed, to question policies and practices, especially for difficulties that were not recognized at the outset.

When someone else defines objectives, goals, and the steps to be taken to reach them, whatever commitment exists will be external. Employees may feel responsible for producing what is required of them, but they will not feel responsible for the way the situation is defined. How can they? They did not do the defining. But so long as the goals are reasonable and the performance requirements specific and fair, most employees will try to meet them. Internal commitment is different. It requires not the acquiescence, but the participation of employees in defining both goals and performance standards.

The more internal commitment is desired, the greater this involvement. But is it realistic to expect thousands of employees to have genuine participation? I think not. One of the most far-reaching programs of employee involvement that I know about—at SmithKline Beecham—created more than four hundred task forces. Yet even this amount of participation did not produce the desired levels of internal commitment. The important thing to keep in mind is the degree of internal commitment that is realistic. Top management risks damaging its credibility if it talks about internal commitment as if there were few limits or—what is far more common—if it espouses internal, but really practices external, commitment.

The differences here are real, and they really matter. Confusion and uncertainty only make things worse. The following exhibit, for example, summarizes the second-order effects of these differences.

EXTERNAL COMMITMENT	INTERNAL COMMITMENT
Perform as required.	Perform as required and keep alert to changing the requirements.
Hold management responsible for defining the work requirements and enabling the employees to achieve them.	Seek joint responsibility for defining work requirements and enabling conditions.
Hold management responsible for identifying and correcting gaps and errors.	Hold themselves responsible for identifying and correcting gaps and errors.
Hold management responsible for defining fair financial compensation.	Seek to influence the definition of financial compensation and seek nonmonetary compensation.
Dependence on management. Be pawns.	Dependence on self. Be originators.
Denies any personal responsibility for choosing external commitment and dependence on management.	Accepts personal responsibility and seeks to choose internal commitment.
Sees inquiry into the way they reason as being unfair, if not a sign of mistrust.	Encourages inquiry into and testing of ideas.
Fears making selves vulnerable lest they will also feel weak.	Seeks making selves vulnerable in ways that they will feel strong.

As noted, difficulties commonly arise when managers espouse values and actions consistent with the right-hand columns but implement programs that are, in fact, consistent with the left. This inner contradiction comes alive largely when implementation efforts begin. Managed poorly, such contradictions can rip an organization apart. Ironically, what often prevents a blowup is that employees learn to live with the inconsistencies by quietly distancing themselves from feeling responsible for continually energizing the programs. This may prevent disaster, but it sacrifices the upside potential of a fully engaged cohort of employees.

No wonder so many reenergizing initiatives have proved disappointing. Notwithstanding the rhetoric of internal commitment, the lower one looks in an organization undergoing reengineering, the more the conditions are consistent with external commitment. This is, no doubt, an important part of the reason why such processes have had, at best, limited positive consequences and, more often, have decreased management's credibility.

For example, the Institute of Management concluded, after a study of 1,100 managers' attitudes (1996), that many companies only pay lip service to internal involvement in decision making. Middle managers (83 percent) favored more involvement, yet their superiors didn't know it. Top managers, the report argues, were not walking the talk, nor were they aware of the credibility gap that they were creating.

Much the same is true of other commitment-focused practices and initiatives. Eccles (1993), for example, in analyzing programs such as the GE "workout" sessions, notes that many of the decisions made were routine—open windows, for example, in an overly hot workspace. When problems were less routine, employees were not empowered to do anything;

decisions and resources remained firmly with top management.

So, too, with many of the practices associated with TQM (total quality management): the espoused theory is consistent with internal commitment, but the reality is more consistent with external commitment. Knights and McCabe (1997), in a review of the literature and of actual TQM-related experience in a bank, conclude that the essential flaw of TQM is that, when implemented, it tends to reinforce the mechanistic and hierarchical models that are consistent with the mental maps of most managers.

Even with the balanced scorecard, as Kaplan and Norton (1996) point out, those at the top who introduce the new methodology are likely to experience conditions akin to internal commitment. But for those involved with implementation at lower levels, the reality is far closer to external commitment.

The same pattern recurs in many discussions and descriptions of enthusiastic program "champions," individuals who can be counted on to:

- Pursue performance objectives with tenacity
- Manage by decree
- Make few compromises while providing generous resources for compliance
- Act as committed defenders
- Keep up the tension: persuade, persuade, persuade
- Monitor frequently: make sure no one strays off course

Even if driven by internal commitment, these behaviors inevitably reinforce the top-down character of the external commitment model. The "one voice" of enthusiastic champions leads to other employees feeling that management is in control and drives out their sense of internal responsibility and personal empowerment. How, in such a circumstance, can they feel personally responsible or empowered? They may be perfectly willing to go along with what is, in reality, a top-down strategy, but the basis for their loyalty and cooperation is external commitment—not the internal commitment preferred by those at the top.

Adler (1993) describes improvement efforts at a plant jointly owned by GM and Toyota. The key lever of change: employees were asked to take responsibility for the analysis of their work, while the engineers who used to perform such activities now acted as consultants to employees. The conditions described by Adler are genuinely consistent with those of internal commitment. Even so, once the work became more routine, feelings changed. As one employee noted, "Working on an assembly line in an automobile factory is still a lousy job."

Now, there is nothing wrong when employees report that they realize there are practical, real-world limits to job redesign. The problem is that management, confusing the two types of commitment, may misattribute such positive outcomes to the effective implementation of their view of empowerment.

This is, in fact, quite common. Garvin (1995) cites the examples of several CEOs who clearly believe that employee focus on predefined, well-executed processes is empowering and liberating:

Paul Allaire (CEO of Xerox):
After all, if you have processes that are in control, you know how the organization is working. There's no guesswork

because variances are small and operating limits are well-defined. . . . You get quality output without a lot of checking.

[and later]

You don't need the old command-and-control approach, which was designated to keep people in line; instead, you can tell people to do their own things provided they respect the process. You wind up with an environment that frees people to be creative. (p. 83)

Craig Weatherup (CEO and President of Pepsi-Cola North America):
I agree with you one thousand percent. A process approach *is* [emphasis is speaker's] liberating. It helps us build reliability and winning consistency, and our people love to win. So over time, they've bought in completely. (p. 83)

Jan Leschly (CEO of SmithKline Beecham):
Sometimes you get the same results by changing the players. . . . It was a gradual process.

[and later]

People have a tough time understanding what it means for processes to be reliable, repeatable, and in control . . . and it will take up years before we can honestly say that all 50,000 people at SmithKline Beecham understand what it means to standardize and improve a process. (p. 83)

But how can there be true empowerment, true internal commitment, when there is no guesswork, when allowable variances are small and operating limits tightly defined?

Because tight controls reduce the need for a lot of checking, employees can feel secure and confident that they will not be unfairly dealt with so long as they follow the dictates of the processes and respect the small variances and operating limits. But this kind of security is empowering only to individuals who have chosen to be pawns. Such people value defined limits precisely because, if they respect them, they will be left alone and not required to question anything. In other words, they are safe from being personally responsible. Such "going by the book" may lead to competent performance, but it neither reflects nor creates internal commitment.

These difficulties and confusions show up, as well, in the hands-on practices of many change professionals whose craft is to facilitate change and continuous learning within an organization. During the past decade, I have had the opportunity to work closely with more than three hundred such professionals, most of whom had had at least eight years of experience. As we worked together, I asked many of them to describe the problems they faced in dealing with gaps and inconsistencies related to internal commitment. Specifically, I asked them to write case studies about their experiences in getting line managers to implement—not back off from efforts to create—genuine participation and internal commitment.

The format was to note, in the right-hand column of a divided page, the actual dialogue (as they remembered it) from some frustrating interaction. And then, in the left-hand columns to describe the thoughts and feelings that they did not express at the time.

THOUGHTS AND FEELINGS NOT EXPRESSED	WHAT I AND THE OTHERS SAID
I better start by getting their views.	**I:** Thanks very much for meeting with me to review our progress in implementing work processes. How would you say things are going? **M1:** Well, I would say that we are meeting all our numbers. **M2:** Yes, but it isn't easy. There is a lot of pressure from above. But we can do it. **M3:** I would agree. Is there something wrong?
I knew he was going to be the big resister.	**I:** Yes, I'm talking about a major change. **M2:** The only kind of changes we do are going to be incremental. Let's be realistic. **M3:** Well, we can't influence very much. I mean it's their managers who will have to tell them.
M3 is so insecure about the things she can influence. I'll try to boost her confidence, later.	**I:** I worry because we all go around talking about collaboration and yet what will happen if the managers say just do it!
I guess it is time to get to the point. Here goes.	**I:** I guess that is my worry. How do we build up the employees' internal commitment? How do we empower them?

Sure you have to do that. But when we started this all of you committed yourselves to integrate the work processes with internal commitment, empowerment, and so on.

I know that you feel I am pressuring, but I am trying to get through to you.

I'm stumped. I feel like I am missing something here. We're almost out of time. I don't want to say something that will reactivate the whole spiral of how they can't do this.

M4: Well, to be honest with you, the clear signals I get from above is that our job is to produce the numbers without, of course, upsetting people. I think that we are doing that.

M6: Yes, do you have information to the contrary?

I: Well, what you are telling me in this session. For example, M3, you said that you expect their local managers to pressure them to meet the numbers. You also say that this isn't going to develop commitments to major types of change. All of you seem to say that change is going to be incremental because that is what is realistic or fits within the scheme of things.

M1: Yes, that's right. Look, please get off my back. I expect to make the numbers especially around quality and customer satisfaction. If your people want to do more on internal commitment and all that stuff, fine. You scheduled those sessions for my people and I'll do my best to make sure they attend.

M4: Yes, we're swamped.

Virtually all the cases follow a similar pattern of diagnosis and action on the part of the change professional:

DIAGNOSIS	ACTION
The line managers are not integrating the hard and soft.	Point out that integration is key and they committed themselves to it.
The line managers are frustrated.	Tell me about your sense of disappointment. What troubles you?
Line managers deny they are disappointed.	Help the line managers see that they are in denial.
Line managers ask to be left alone to implement the work processes.	Let's work together. They don't really understand how to integrate.
Line managers are reneging on their commitment.	Deny their views of disappointment and begin to become more directive and controlling.

Seen in context, these responses primarily work to deflect the real issues or escape from them through abstraction. The change professionals started and ended feeling that the line managers were too numbers-oriented; the line managers, that the "soft" change professionals did not realize the reality they had to face. In the name of maintaining a good working relationship, all parties bypassed and then covered up their bypass. The inevitable result: inner contradictions remain and frustration grows. Thus, gaps and inconsistencies are not just problems of logic or argument. They are a recipe, a tested recipe, for bickering, dysfunctional behavior, and lackluster performance.

Further Reading

Reengineering: Clemons, Row, and Thatcher 1995; Grint and Case 1998; Hendry 1995; Jackson 1996; Stoddard, Jarvenpaa, and Littlejohn 1996; White and Wolf 1995.

TQM: Hackman and Wageman 1995; Knights and McCabe 1997; Mazen 1997; Sitkin, Sutcliffe, and Schroeder 1994.

Participation and Empowerment: Eccles 1993; Heller, Pusic, Strauss, and Wilpert 1998; Meyer and Allen 1997; Mohrman, Galbraith, and Lawler 1998; Wilkinson 1998.

New Perspectives on Human Resources: Lawler 1996; Legge 1995.

Human Resources in Building Competitive Edge Leaders: Ulrich, Losey, and Lake 1997.

3

Why Flawed Advice Persists

CHAPTERS 1 AND 2 SURFACE A PUZZLE: if so much professional advice, even if implemented correctly, leads to consequences that are counterproductive because of the inconsistencies and gaps it contains, why have so many users found that advice to be helpful? Solving this puzzle is more important than we might initially realize. Something powerful and fundamental is going on here—something that goes right to the heart of what I think of as the theory of action.

Let me begin with an obvious premise: human action is produced by human beings using their mind/brain. No meaningful action is possible without an internally consistent design, script, or scenario that specifies—for a given set of conditions and a given set of governing values—intended outcomes, as well as the actual behaviors required to produce those outcomes. Thus, the heart of each design is a causal claim: if we act in such and such a way, the intended consequences will likely occur, subject to the constraints of the underlying values.

Good designs pave the way for effective action—that is, action that leads to the intended consequences with few, if any, counterproductive side effects. If any such side effects do occur, they must be specified ahead of time. Moreover, the results of effective action persevere and do not harm whatever level of effectiveness currently exists. Implicit in this definition is the further requirement that all actions should be monitored to see if they are leading to their intended results.

Advice of the sort under discussion is just a proposed design or script for action. As such, the causal claims embedded in advice can be tested and should, therefore, be crafted in ways that allow them to be tested. These tests should be as robust as possible to reduce, if not eliminate, all sources of error. And they should be implementable in everyday life; otherwise they cannot be of much help to those taking action.

Perhaps an example, drawn from my consulting work, will help bring these points to life. The chief information officer (CIO) of a large electronics firm was told by the CEO that an important organizational problem existed and had to be corrected.* The problem was that the Information Technology (IT) group was too large and too expensive. Moreover, its service to the line organization was inadequate.

The CEO reminded the CIO that this was not the first time he had spoken of this problem. He was becoming impatient. He warned that if costs did not go down and if the quality and efficiency of service did not improve, he would be forced to take drastic action that might include finding a new CIO.

Not surprisingly, the CIO called a meeting of his immediate reports to take corrective action. He began the session by

---

* This section borrows heavily from Argyris and Schön 1997, pp. 88–103, 111–120.

telling his subordinates that he had received a "read-our-lips" message from line management: cooperation from IT was nonexistent, and IT professionals were providing minimal value added, despite ever-higher budgets. "Therefore," he said, "I want to discuss with you our ability to react to users' needs. We are always having difficulties with line management. But they are, after all, our customers. We have to be concerned about meeting their needs."

Members of the IT group responded, "We *are* concerned about their needs. The big trouble is that they do not know what they want. On the rare occasions they do, they have no idea how long it will take us to provide them with high-quality services. They always want everything yesterday. We have had it up to here with their complaints. The problem could be easily solved if they gave us the people and resources we truly need."

The CIO expressed empathy with the IT group's frustration and anger and suggested that they might begin to turn things around by developing what he called a "credible plan to respond to [customer] needs." Their response was brief and bitter: "There is no sense in planning; our users don't plan. They demand and complain. Whenever we think we are on top of things, they make new demands and complain about what we are failing to do."

The CIO tried again: "Since we do not have a solid plan, we cannot review the way we are managing our resources. . . . As I see it, we have two choices. The first is to continue to do what we are doing—and I believe that will be disastrous. The second is to break out of this mold and change the way we do business."

Members of the group countered by arguing that there was no way to change line management. As one put it, "If you want to try, good luck." The CIO replied, "If planning isn't the way to go, how do you propose to solve the problem?"

The IT professionals responded with increasing emotion, arguing, in effect, that (1) the problem was not solvable because line management makes impossible requests; and (2) the IT professionals were already killing themselves. "That's why the good people are leaving," said one individual. "I agree," said another. "It is not fixable."

Virtually at the end of his patience, the CIO finally exclaimed, "We have to fix it because we have no choice! Otherwise we are not being responsible."

Clearly, the IT professionals are expressing frustration with—and mistrust of—both line executives and their own superior. As a result, they craft their conversation in a way that makes productive dialogue difficult. For example, they advocate their positions and make evaluations and attributions about line management in ways that neither encourage nor permit inquiry or testing:

- The line does not know what it wants.
- The line makes demands with unrealistic deadlines.
- If we meet their demands, they will follow up with more unrealistic demands.
- These problems are unfixable because of line management's recalcitrance.

Now, the CIO wanted to get his subordinates to be cooperative. He also wanted to minimize the likelihood that they would see him as unfair and judgmental. So, unlike his subordinates, he censored his evaluations and attributions and then acted as if this were not the case. Asked to write out his private thoughts and feelings, he offered the following:

- These guys act like a bunch of babies.
- They do not realize how insensitive and opinionated they are.
- Sometimes I feel that I should read the riot act to them. They've got to wise up or all of us will lose.

When asked what led him not to make these thoughts and feelings public, he looked astonished. "If I said this stuff, all it would do is add fuel to the fire." He was correct. His private thoughts and feelings were crafted in the same counterproductive manner as were his and his subordinates' public conversation.

The use of self-induced censorship to create conditions for dialogue is rarely successful. When, for example, members of the IT group were asked if they had any idea of their boss's private thoughts, they responded with words that were almost identical to the ones the CIO had actually used. When they were asked what led them not to say them aloud, they responded with the same look of astonishment. "Are you kidding," said one. "That would make things worse." Quite likely, they were also carrying on internal monologues that were not vocalized. Thus, we have people holding private conversations about each other and thinking that the others did not hear those conversations. In actuality, they did "hear" them, but acted as if they did not.

As I saw it, the CIO had begun the meeting with a "take

charge" attitude. He told his group about negative evaluations by the top, warned them that the time had come for corrective action, and requested a constructive dialogue about what could be done to correct the situation. But the subordinates also had their own "take charge" attitude. They bypassed the CIO's requests, arguing that the problems were caused by line management.

The CIO responded in two ways. First, he avoided publicly expressing his negative feelings, fearing that doing so would make the situation worse. He was right. If he had made public his negative evaluations and attributions, he would likely have activated the same kind of defensiveness that his subordinates' negative evaluations and attributions had activated in him. The very way he framed his private thoughts and feelings was counterproductive to learning. The irony was that his private thoughts were consistent with the views of the CEO. Both saw the IT professionals as uncooperative and acting childishly.

The unintended result: in the name of producing a positive dialogue, the CIO increased the amount of information that was withheld, suppressed his personal feelings, bypassed the feelings of his subordinates, and acted as if he were not doing so. Then, when the CIO asked the group to develop a rational, credible plan for responding to the needs of line management, they rejected the suggestion on the grounds that it was irrational. Line managers, they agreed, did not know how to plan and would only escalate their demands and criticisms.

The structure here is interesting. All participants seem to have the same strategy: all believe that they should take charge and warn the others that their actions are not acceptable. But, in practice, this activates a barrage of evaluations and attributions, which are crafted in ways that do not encourage learning. For example, the subordinates evaluate the line as unable to plan and attribute to them the intention of making life difficult for the IT group. The CIO privately feels the same about the IT group, but decides that he should suppress his private thoughts and feelings to avoid provoking unconstructive emotional responses and focus, instead, on developing rational new plans.

This strategy fails to achieve its intended objectives. The subordinates respond with even more emotion and make more negative evaluations and attributions, which they communicate with a sense of rising certainty. (If the CIO had asked them openly how they knew their diagnosis was correct, they would probably have said, "Trust us, we work with them, we know!") Then, when some of the professionals were asked if they had any idea of their boss's private thoughts, they used words that were almost identical to the ones the CIO used about himself. And when asked what led them not to discuss their views, one of them said, "That would make things worse. All you would get is a blowup." Like the CIO, the subordinates were carrying on private conversations, making private attributions, and covering up the fact they were doing so.

Reflecting on these consequences, it seems fair to infer the following: all the participants experienced an interest in solving the business problem, but their ways of crafting their conversation, combined with their self-censorship, led to a dialogue that was defensive and self-reinforcing. When this kind of impasse occurs, everyone has to focus on two major problems:

1. The business problem they set out to solve in the first place.
2. The problem triggered by defensiveness, mistrust, its cover-up, and the cover-up of the cover-up.

The latter problem, we suggest, takes up a lot of all participants' span of attention. Not only do they have to listen to the other parties and think about their response; they must also strive to do this while, at the same time, keeping track of their cover-ups.

Remember where we started: a business problem identified as high IT costs and poor IT performance. Everyone agreed with this description of the problem, but disagreed about its causes. The CIO then went into his meeting with three assumptions about the action strategies he should adopt in order to make the meeting effective:

1. I should take charge of the meeting if it is to meet my objectives. My definition of victory is that my subordinates develop a plan that will convince senior line executives that they intend to cut costs.
2. It is important for me to involve my subordinates in developing a corrective plan. They will then be more committed to its implementation.
3. If my subordinates become emotional and do not act like grown-ups, I must suppress my feelings about the latter and defuse my reaction to the former by focusing on rational actions, such as planning. The way to suppress my negative feelings is to experience them privately, censor them from the group, and act as if I were not doing so.

The IT group used action strategies based on similar assumptions. They, too, felt that they should take charge of the meeting. Their definition of victory was that the CIO would realize that the major obstacle to solving the problem was the line managers. They, too, sought to involve the CIO so that he would become a more effective spokesman for their views with top management. Finally, they assumed that their responses were rational. Whenever they added emotional decibels, it was to make sure that the CIO heard what they said.

These shared strategies and assumptions led each side to craft conversations that upset the other, which led, in turn, to bypassing the emotional dimensions of important issues, which then became undiscussable. A conversation that is intended to be positive actually produces defensive reactions in all participants, who deal with these defensive reactions in ways that—with the best intentions—reinforce and escalate defensiveness.

This self-reinforcing pattern of action strategy and anti-learning consequence is what I call a primary inhibitory loop. Such loops are "primary" in the sense that they are informed by the participants' theories-in-use during face-to-face discussions, especially when the discussions are laced with embarrassment or threat. Within such loops, responses that are defensive and dysfunctional get triggered by and, in turn, reinforce conditions for error. Not being able to discuss important issues is one example; others include vagueness and ambiguity in what gets said or implied.

In the CIO's meeting with his subordinates, the actual causes of line/staff troubles remain both vague (they are neither clearly specified nor illustrated) and ambiguous (the different interpretations are neither clarified nor resolved). Attributions that the CIO and his subordinates make about each other or about line management remain untested. Worse, to the extent that they cannot be tested so long as the feelings associated with them are undiscussable, they become untestable.

In organizational settings, when conditions for error set off defensive reactions like those of the CIO and his subordinates, these reactions, in turn, reduce the likelihood that individuals will engage in the kind of fair and open inquiry that leads to productive outcomes. Vagueness and ambiguity often yield organizational situations that individual members find threatening. So does uncertainty about what is to be done and by whom, or about criteria for performance. And so does the withholding of important information or the de facto treatment of important issues as undiscussable.

These defensive patterns are painfully familiar. Few managers will find their existence newsworthy. Why, then, do the counterproductive dialogues in which they are embedded occur so systematically? And why do they persist? No one wants them. Texts and courses on organization design, leadership, conflict resolution, and employee empowerment treat these loops as violating both the letter and the spirit of modern management and organization theory. But persist they do.

Part of the answer is related to the assumptions and skills individuals learn to use early in life in dealing with issues that are embarrassing and threatening. But individuals are only part of the answer. Part of it has to do with the way organizations behave. And still another part involves the interactions between organization and individual. Let me begin with the individual.

People hold two different "theories of action" about effective behavior: the one they espouse and the one they actually use. When they deal with issues that are embarrassing or threatening, their reasoning and action conform to a type of theory-in-use that I call Model I. Model I generates the kinds of primary loops described above. In the case cited, neither the CIO nor his subordinates espoused such a theory of action, yet all of them used it.

In Model I, the core injunctions that people strive to satisfy through their actions include:

1. *Define goals and try to achieve them*—that is, not try to develop, with others, a mutual definition of shared purpose.
2. *Maximize winning and minimize losing*—that is, treating any change in goals, once they are decided on, as a sign of weakness.
3. *Minimize the generation or expression of negative feelings*—which would be interpreted as showing ineptness, incompetence, or lack of diplomacy.
4. Be rational—that is, remaining objective and intellectual and suppressing feelings.

To accomplish these ends, under Model I, people will seek to:

1. *Design and manage the environment unilaterally*—that is, plan actions secretly and persuade or cajole others to agree with one's definition of the situation.
2. *Own and control the task.*
3. *Unilaterally protect yourself*—that is, keep yourself from being vulnerable by speaking in abstractions, avoiding

reference to directly observed events, and withholding underlying thoughts and feelings.

4. *Unilaterally protect others from being hurt*—in particular, by withholding important information, telling white lies, suppressing feelings, and offering false sympathy. Moreover, do not test the assumption that the other person needs to be protected or that the strategy of protection should be kept secret.

Following any of these action strategies means behaving unilaterally toward others and protectively toward oneself. If successful, such behavior controls others and prevents one from being controlled by them. But at a stiff price: being seen as defensive and willing to have relations with others colored by mistrust and rigidity.

No wonder there is little public testing of the assumptions embedded in such theories-in-use. As with the CIO and his group, testing would require confronting one's own defensiveness, as well as the defensiveness of others. This means, in practice, that much action will be based on an untested theory-in-use, which then inevitably becomes self-sealing—that is, immersed in a closed, self-reinforcing defensive loop.

In an earlier book, *Theory in Practice* (1974), Don Schön and I describe how lack of public testing risks creating self-sealing processes. The individual not only helps to create behavioral worlds that are artifacts of his theory-in-use but also cuts himself off from the possibility of disconfirming assumptions in his theory-in-use and, thus, from the possibility of helping to create behavioral worlds that disconfirm his starting assumptions about them.

However, public testing of theories-in-use must be accompanied by an openness to changing behavior as a function of learning. The actor needs minimally distorted feedback from others. If others provide such feedback—especially if they do so with some risk—and if they experience that the actor is not open to change, they may believe that they have placed themselves in a difficult situation. Their mistrust of the actor will probably increase, but this fact will be suppressed. The result will be the creation of another series of self-sealing processes that again make the actor less likely to receive valid information the next time he tries to test an assumption publicly (p. 78).

Because effective learning depends on both the exchange of valid information and the public testing of attributions and assumptions, Model I tends to discourage it. Because long-term effectiveness depends on the possibility of such learning, Model I tends toward long-term ineffectiveness.

This, too is a self-reinforcing process. In a world of defensiveness and escalating error, it is understandable that people will try to protect themselves by striving even harder to be in unilateral control, to win and not lose, to deal with the defensiveness of others by attempting to be—and encouraging others to be—"rational," and to suppress, as best they can, their own and others' negative feelings. And this, in turn, means that social values such as concern, caring, honesty, strength, and courage will likely become defined in ways that support Model I theory-in-use. Concern and caring, for example, will come to mean: "Act diplomatically; say only things that people want to hear." In much the same way, strength will come to mean winning, maintaining unilateral control of a situation, and keeping private one's feelings of vulnerability.

As this dysfunctional cycle locks into place, people become

highly skilled in their execution of Model I strategies. Their actions will "work"—in that they achieve their intended objectives while appearing spontaneous, automatic, and effortless. As a result, the people in question will be even less likely to reflect on, learn about, or modify their Model I behavior.

Secondary inhibitory loops refer to the behavioral loops— the causal connections between action strategies and their anti-learning consequences—related to the interactions of groups within organizations. Figure 3.1 maps—for the CIO example—the pattern of relationships among primary and secondary loops, beginning with the governing conditions that set these patterns in motion: the dissatisfactions of users and the tight financial conditions that no longer permit high IT costs.

Next come the action strategies the CIO and his subordinates used during their meeting and their first-order consequences. One such consequence, of course, was that the CIO evaluated the group's conclusions as unrealistic and challenged them to come up with something better. The group then evaluated the CIO's solution as unrealistic and said that the problem would remain unsolvable unless line management changed. These interactions led to second-order consequences in the form of two sets of double binds—one affecting the group, the other affecting the CIO as well as line managers had they been present.

Here lies the transition from primary to secondary loops. Line managers judge IT staff as unrealistic and lacking in cost-consciousness; the staff judges the underlying problems to be the responsibility of line managers themselves. Both views become embedded in the organizational norms that govern relationships between line and staff.

Figure 3.1 Perseverance of Counterproductive Actions and Attitudes

Governing Conditions	Action Strategies	Consequences			
		First Order	Second Order	Third Order	Fourth Order
Pressures from users	**Boss** Make attributions and evaluations Reactive Defeatist Poor performance Make attributions and evaluations untestable	Unrealistic solutions Come up with a better solution or use mine	Double bind: Either agree with me or feel failure *or* Do not agree with me or feel failure	Undiscussable Steadfast, unmoving	Self-reinforcing Self-sealing Mistrust Cynicism Low confidence
Tight financial resources	**Subordinates** Make attributions and evaluations: Bosses and users are unfair Do not care for MIS professionals Do not understand Use brute force to win Make attributions and evaluations untestable	Unrealistic solutions Problem is unsolvable Users and boss are at fault	Double bind: Agree with us and get in trouble with users *or* Cooperate with them and get in trouble with us		

The double binds that follow from such judgments and norms feed into a pattern of intergroup conflict typical of line–staff relationships. Also typical is the fact that these conflicts become undiscussable, and their not being discussed becomes undiscussable. Each group sees the other as unmovable, and both see the problem as correctable—if only the other side would change its behavior.

All this feeds back to reinforce the primary loops at work in the CIO's meeting with his subordinates, creating an organizational pattern that "seals in" the whole counterproductive cycle. Inevitably, each participant feels mistrust of the others, low confidence in interactions with the others, and cynicism about the likelihood of resolving conflicts with the others. These feelings are legitimized because they are seen as typical of the organization.

As Figure 3.1 shows, any dialogue about the business problem of reducing IT's costs and improving its performance will be negatively influenced by these primary and secondary inhibitory loops. If line managers are unaware of interactions captured on the map because they have been shielded from them, they will see only the persistence of high costs and poor performance. Understandably, this leads them to mistrust the CIO and feel doubt, even cynicism, about his ability to solve the business problem. (As it turned out, the CIO in the case was eventually fired and replaced by a "tough line officer.") But even if managers had not been shielded, they would—without some change in the structure of belief and action—probably still have had the same kind of reaction.

Such changes do not come easily. This is, in large part, because the patterns described both create and sustain organizational defensive routines. These routines are made up of actions and policies within an organizational setting that are intended to protect individuals from experiencing embarrassment or threat, while at the same time preventing them, as well as the organization as a whole, from identifying the causes of the embarrassment or threat, while at the same time preventing them, as well as the organization as a whole, from identifying the causes of the embarrassment or threat in order to correct them.

All such routines are based on a logic that is powerful and profound in its impact on individuals and organizations. The logic can be expressed in terms of four rules:

1. Craft messages that contain ambiguities or inconsistencies.
2. Act as if the messages were not inconsistent.
3. Make the ambiguity and inconsistency in the message undiscussable.
4. Make this undiscussability undiscussable.

Think, for example, of a chief executive who says to her immediate subordinates, "We encourage everyone to be innovative and risk-oriented. This is what we mean by empowerment. Of course, we also expect you to keep out of trouble."

This is, of course, a classic mixed message. People usually send mixed messages spontaneously, with no indication that the message is mixed. If they appeared to hesitate because of the inconsistencies in the message, others might see it as a sign of weakness. It is rare, indeed, for an executive to send a mixed message and then ask, "Do you find my message inconsistent or ambiguous?" The nature of the message is made undiscussable by the very naturalness with which it is delivered, by the absence of any invitation or disposition to inquire about it, and by the undiscussability of its undiscussability.

People follow such rules all the time. They do so without having to pay much attention to them because they have become highly skilled at enacting them. The irony is that this skillfulness is inextricably linked with incompetence in that the skillful use of mixed messages leads to a range of unintended and counterproductive consequences. The CIO and his subordinates created a dialogue in which crucial messages were covered up, and the cover-up was not discussable. This led to increasing emotionality, as well as to double binds, which then led to—or reinforced—feelings of mistrust, cynicism, and lack of confidence in the other parties to the dialogue.

It is simply not possible to deal effectively with any subject if it is not discussable and if its undiscussability is not discussable. Thus, under the rules that govern defensive routines, individuals with a high sense of integrity and a willingness to accept personal responsibility will feel that they are in the following double bind: If we do not discuss the defensive routines, then these routines will continue to proliferate. But if we do discuss them, we are likely to get into trouble. According to one colorful senior executive, in his organization these double binds go under the name of "s—— sandwiches."

Double binds matter because they allow defensive routines to be protected and reinforced by the very people who would most like to get rid of them. This protection is covert and undiscussable, which makes the routines appear self-protective and self-reinforcing. And whenever actions are self-protective and self-reinforcing, they can easily become self-proliferating. The irony here is that the self-proliferating features of

defensive routines are triggered most powerfully when someone tries to engage them directly. Once individuals realize that
danger, they shy away from engagement in the name of
progress and constructive action.

Under these conditions, defensive routines flourish and
spread into organizational loops that are known to all and
manageable by none. Indeed, executives have often told us
that the very thought that defensive loops *could* be managed
is unrealistic, futile, and romantic. A few have wondered if
such management might not actually be dangerous because,
as one put it, "Wouldn't it mean that we would have to give up
whatever we have to protect us?"

These reactions make sense in the world as it is. They are
also self-fulfilling and self-sealing—self-fulfilling, because they
create the conditions under which it would be naïve or dangerous to engage them; self-sealing, because they also create
the conditions under which it is unlikely that the self-fulfilling
prophecy will be interrupted.

Here, then, is one of the most important causes of organizational rigidity and stickiness: defensive routines inexorably get
stronger and stronger while the individuals responsible for
them believe it is unrealistic or even dangerous to do much
about them. Since these routines are accepted as inevitable,
natural, and immune to management or influence, it is not
surprising that the most common reaction to them is a sense
of helplessness.

Employees in industrialized societies appear as fatalistic
about them as peasants are about poverty. People do not take
responsibility for creating or maintaining them. They are willing to say that they are personally influenced by them, but are

unable or unwilling to see how they might create or reinforce them. They do, however, develop a cynical attitude about them: "Nothing will ever change around here."

Because cynicism makes it easy to ignore or sneer at evidence of positive intentions, cynical people automatically mistrust others and see the world as full of evidence that nothing will change. It is a short step from this kind of attitude to blaming other people in an organization for any difficulties that may arise.

There will always be plenty of evidence that someone else is to blame, that defensive loops exist, and that others are both acting consistently with them and covering up the fact that they are. Even when the cynics try to be positive and constructive, their advice often reinforces defensive routines. "Be careful," they warn. "You'll get yourself in trouble if you try to change that: it's a legacy from way back." In other words, respect the defensive routines and inhibitory loops that make it so difficult for people to take constructive action in the first place.

Organizations whose people operate with Model I theories-in-use will create behavioral worlds and learning environments that are consistent with Model I. Such worlds and environments are highly unlikely to alter their governing variables, norms, or assumptions spontaneously because doing so would require unwelcome and uncomfortable inquiry into inhibitory loops. They can, as a result, rarely change—unaided—from within.

They need at least an approximate picture of a new end state to aim toward, a map of how to move there from Model I, and warning signs of the kinds of behaviors (making statements that are not disconfirmable, for example, or unilaterally controlling others in order to win) that would knock such movement off course. But they also need rules in the form of maxims or heuristics to help them create genuine Model II behaviors, like advocating a position and coupling it with inquiry, making private dilemmas public, and framing attributions so that they can de disconfirmed.

In a Model II environment, the action theory-in-use helps—indeed, requires—mistaken assumptions to be reformulated, incongruities reconciled, incompatibilities resolved, vagueness specified, untestable notions made testable, scattered information brought together into meaningful patterns, and previously withheld information shared. These are the kinds of conditions that favor productive dialogue, not those that trigger, as with Model I, inhibitory loops.

What kind of conversation would the CIO described earlier create if his objective, consistent with Model II, were to reduce interpersonal and organizational defenses and the conditions for error? First, he would carry on a private conversation in which he pushed to make issues more explicit and tested the validity of assumptions and attributions. Thus, when he heard his subordinates say that line managers "do not know what they want," he might say to himself:

> These individuals are making evaluations of—and attributions about—the line's intentions without providing any data that I could use to make up my own mind about the validity of their claims. I should ask them to provide data to illustrate their claims. I have learned not to ask them "why" they believe what they do because that will activate espoused-theory explanations that are likely to be self-serving. That means, when they

say that line managers don't know what they want, I should say, "What is it that they say or do that leads you to conclude that they do not know what they want?"

If this question gets answered with concrete information, the CIO can make a judgment as to whether line managers really are acting inappropriately. If he believes they are, he can communicate these evaluations upward in order to begin to change the line managers' actions.

Similarly, when his subordinates say that the line does not trust them or really care for them, the CIO could say, "Have you tested your assumptions about their views of us? If so, what did you say to the line? If not, what led you not to do so?"

If the CIO asks these questions, the group might respond, "Are you kidding? That would be disastrous. They would either laugh or get furious." This response is, of course, yet another attribution about line management. As such, it can—and should—moreover, be tested by a logic different from that which initially produced it. So, if all the CIO hears are further untested assertions, he could say, "I asked if you tested the validity of your assertions about the line. The answer I get is another set of untested assertions. This is not good enough. I cannot be an effective representative of our views with line management if I come to the meetings armed only with untestable assertions."

If the CIO hears what he believes are incorrect or self-sealing conclusions, he could ask:

If it is true that the users are the problem because they do not plan and do make last-minute demands, and if it is also true that they have been doing this for years, wouldn't giving us increased resources reinforce the very behavior we find frustrating?

The CIO could also cite actions that illustrate how his group might be creating the very consequences they condemn. He might, for instance, say:

> You stated that our customers are inflexible and insensitive. You do not like this behavior, and you use it as evidence that the problems are not correctable. You may be right, but I do not hear anyone presenting a compelling argument that is also testable. Whenever I have tried to make some suggestions, the responses that I hear from you include 'good luck to you' and 'trust us, our users are uninfluenceable.' It is difficult for me to trust this kind of diagnosis. If you act toward the line managers the way you are acting toward me, I can see how they would become, in your eyes, uninfluenceable. But I can also see how they may come to a similar conclusion about you.

or

> This leads me to another issue. You may be finding me uninfluenceable. I want to establish conversations that do not require me to distance myself from my responsibility or yours for the problems we are experiencing. I want to explore what I am saying or doing that makes me, in your eyes, uninfluenceable.

The scenarios I have just presented are informed by the model for *individual* theory-in-use that I call Model II (Argyris and Schön, 1974, pp. 85–93). The governing variables or values of Model II—valid information, free and informed choice,

Figure 3.2 Model I, Theory-in-use

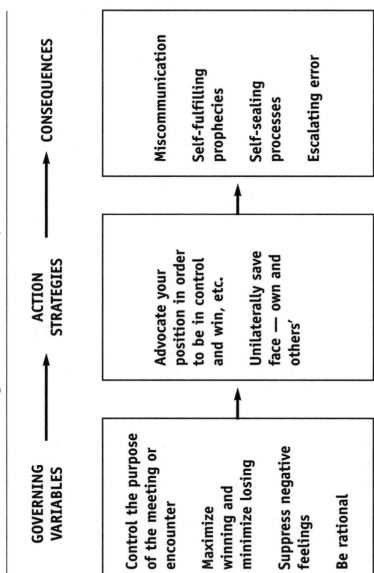

GOVERNING
VARIABLES

ACTION
STRATEGIES

CONSEQUENCES

Control the purpose
of the meeting or
encounter

Maximize
winning and
minimize losing

Suppress negative
feelings

Be rational

Advocate your
position in order
to be in control
and win, etc.

Unilaterally save
face — own and
others'

Miscommunication

Self-fulfilling
prophecies

Self-sealing
processes

Escalating error

and internal commitment—are not, however, opposite those of Model I. Nor are the action strategies required to fulfill these values opposite those of Model I. In Model I, individuals advocate their purposes and simultaneously try to control others and the environment to assure that those purposes are achieved (Figure 3.2). Model II does not reject the skill or competence to advocate one's purposes. But it does reject the unilateral control that usually accompanies advocacy because the typical purpose of advocacy is to win.

In other words, Model II couples articulateness and advocacy with an invitation to others to confront the views and emotions of both self and other. It seeks to alter views in order to base them on the most complete and valid information possible and construct positions to which the people involved can become internally committed. And it invites double-loop learning on the part of others. Every significant Model II action is evaluated in terms of the degree to which it helps the individuals involved generate valid and useful information (including relevant feelings), share a problem in ways that lead to productive inquiry, solve the problem such that it remains solved, and do so without reducing the present level of problem-solving effectiveness.

The behavioral strategies of Model II involve sharing power with anyone who has competence and is relevant to deciding about implementing the action in question. Definition of the task and control over the environment are shared with all the relevant actors. Saving one's own face or that of others is resisted as a defensive, anti-learning activity. On those occasions when face-saving actions must be taken, they are planned jointly with the people involved.

Under these conditions individuals will not tend to

Figure 3.3 Model II, Theory-in-use

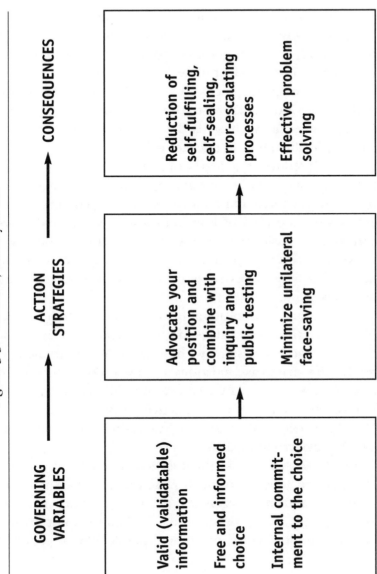

GOVERNING VARIABLES → ACTION STRATEGIES → CONSEQUENCES

Valid (validatable) information

Free and informed choice

Internal commit-ment to the choice

Advocate your position and combine with inquiry and public testing

Minimize unilateral face-saving

Reduction of self-fulfilling, self-sealing, error-escalating processes

Effective problem solving

compete to make decisions for others, to one-up each other, or to outshine others for the purpose of self-gratification. They will, instead, seek to find the people most competent to make the decision or solve the problem at hand. And they will build viable decision-making networks, in which the major function of the group is to maximize the contributions of each member so that, when a synthesis is developed, it incorporates the widest possible range of relevant views (see Figure 3.3).

Model II reduces the degree of defensiveness in individuals, within groups, and among groups at the same time that it boosts free choice and feelings of internal commitment. It emphasizes the kind of learning through which individuals confront the basic assumptions behind their own and others' views and through which they seek public tests of their underlying hypotheses so as to make them disconfirmable, not self-sealing.

There is another collateral benefit of using Model II theories-in-use. The social values in good currency today are, for the most part, consistent with Model I. When applied correctly, they may make individuals feel good or righteous, but they are also likely to exacerbate conditions for error and reduce the chance for productive organizational inquiry. Model II versions of these social values have a far different— and, I think—vastly superior effect.

This brings us back to the question posed at the outset of this chapter: why, if so much professional advice is riddled with gaps and inconsistencies, do users continue to find it helpful? True, it may produce, more often than not, frustrating and unsatisfactory outcomes. But it allows people to

HELP AND SUPPORT

Give approval and praise to others. Tell others what you believe will make them feel good about themselves. Reduce their feelings of hurt by telling them how much you care and, if possible, agree with them that the others acted improperly.

RESPECT FOR OTHERS

Defer to other people; do not confront their reasoning or actions.

STRENGTH

Advocate your position in order to win. Hold your own position in the face of advocacy. Feeling vulnerable is a sign of weakness.

HELP AND SUPPORT

Increase the others' capacity to confront their own ideas, to create a window into their own mind, and to face the unsurfaced assumptions, biases, and fears that have informed their actions toward other people.

RESPECT FOR OTHERS

Attribute to other people a high capacity for self-reflection and self-examination without becoming so upset that they lose their effectiveness and their sense of self-responsibility and choice. Keep testing this attribution.

STRENGTH

Advocate your position and combine it with inquiry and self-reflection. Feeling vulnerable while encouraging inquiry is a sign of strength.

HONESTY	**HONESTY**
Tell other people no lies, or tell others all you think and feel.	Encourage yourself and other people to make public tests of their ability to say what they know yet fear to say. Minimize what would otherwise be subject to distortion and cover-up of the distortion.
INTEGRITY	**INTEGRITY**
Stick to your principles, values, and beliefs.	Advocate your principles, values, and beliefs in a way that invites inquiry into them and encourages other people to do the same.

remain within the comfort zone defined by Model I versions of deeply held social values—and, by so doing, tacitly encourages them to place primary responsibility for unwelcome outcomes *not* on systematic faults in the advice being used, but on intractable realities "out there." When "accept it, that's just the way it is and has always been" is widely treated as a perfectly legitimate explanation of failure, there is no felt need to look for micro-level causes closer to home. After all, how can any individual—or any piece of advice—be held to account for the intransigence of the universe?

But, if we are honest, we know that higher levels of performance that this are possible, even if uncomfortable to reach.

And we know that the results of the advice often followed are really not okay. If errors are actions and if actions are designed, then all errors not due to simple ignorance must also be designed. We can change the design.

In the cases cited in previous chapters, for example, Katzenback's real change leaders were trying to remain in control, to win and not lose, and to skirt negative feelings by "being positive." Similarly, Covey's actions with his son, whatever his espoused theory, involved hiding his frustration and his feelings—and then covering up that he was doing so. In both instances, worry about the negative impact of being candid and honest led to a pattern of well-intended "easing in," which is not consistent with Model II.

Covey, remember, gave his son approval and praise, strove to say what he thought would make him feel good, and expressed genuine caring and concern—all this, while having increasingly negative feelings about his actions. By contrast, Model II dialogue would have worked to increase the son's capacity to face up to his own commitments and reflect on his own assumptions, biases, and reasoning. The conscious intent of "easing in" may be to express respect by deferring to, not confronting, another's reasoning or actions. But it ultimately leads to a lower degree of trust because it assumes that the other has a low capacity for self-reflection and self-examination. Although comfortable, Model I limits learning and puts a ceiling on both personal growth and group performance.

4

Human Resources Practices

IN MANY COMPANIES, the Human Resources (HR) function has the responsibility for developing the framework for producing non-routine, transformational policies and practices related to leadership, learning, change, and commitment. By and large, they not only implement this responsibility poorly; they actually make the situation worse. The professionals who are supposed to be leaders are, at best, keepers of the status quo and, at worse, drivers of the low effectiveness of their programs.

"Tom" was a corporate figure representative of some three hundred change professionals. Tom, like the individuals for whom he stands, had regularly met resistance from line managers, which he regarded as a betrayal of the agreements they had made at the outset. As Tom's case illustrates, when these professionals were confronted with such reactions, they acted consistently with Model I theory-in-use and Model I social values. This only strengthened their organizations' defensive routines.

Similarly, programs such as reengineering and total quality management are often introduced by processes that reduce the likelihood of creating internal commitment among employees. Certainly, a vision→strategy→process→individual roles approach is a rational framework for implementing these programs. But it leads to external commitment, although the "selling" language is all about internal commitment.

In many instances, HR professionals bypassed these inconsistencies and acted as if they were not doing so—and then covered up the bypass and made the cover-up undiscussable. As a result, their theory-in-use was consistent with the one that they advised should not be used. No wonder they often appear ineffective; no wonder line managers often question their credibility.

During the past five years I have been using the "Tom" case in workshops for experienced HR experts, many from large corporations that are highly regarded for their HR policies and practices. Here are several excerpts from the tape recordings of these sessions:

> I think the key (for Tom) is not to respond, but to be responsive.

> Yes, I agree. Tom should try to develop, in some kind of a conversation, a real sense of what the survival issues are for the client.

> Yes, and help the client to feel that all is not lost.

> These are some ways that working to get this can really build some shared view of what it is that might be possible.

. . . and try to frame that in terms that are pretty understandable for folks (which it is difficult to do) to connect directly to
business performance.

Let us reflect for a moment on these contributions. They
are crafted in ways that are similar to much of the advice
described in Chapters 1 and 3:

1. The advice is phrased in terms of end results: be responsive, develop a real sense of the survival issue, encourage the client not to feel lost, and craft the conversation
   in understandable language.
2. The contributions do not specify what Tom might say to
   produce these end results.
3. The end results are not specified in ways that are operational. For example, what is the difference between
   responding versus being responsive? What is the nature
   of "some kind of conversation" or building "shared
   views" of what is possible? And what is "understandable
   language"?
4. The causal theory in each bit of advice is not made
   explicit. This makes it difficult to test the validity of
   these claims without using self-referential, self-sealing
   logic. The speakers do not appear to see the necessity
   for a test of the validity of their advice, much less the
   need to formulate one that is independent of their logic.

Implicit in all this advice is a "mini" causal theory that I
tested in several specific conversations. The theory goes
something like this: if Tom develops a real sense of the issues
around client survival, if he assures the clients that all is not
lost, if he asks the clients to work to build a shared view of

their wishes, if he does all this in an understandable way, then and only then will he be able to help the line make progress toward genuine integration and commitment.

The HR group members agreed that this framing was a valid representation of the causal assumptions behind their advice. This led us to the issue of abstractness and end results. I said that key terms in this causal logic were "real sense," "assure," "share," and "understandable language." How would they implement abstract terms like these?

I requested that they answer this question by producing the actual conversation that they would use in helping Tom. I would play the role of the line managers. I asked the group members to monitor my role play vigilantly and to interrupt if they thought that I was being unfair or too tough.

HR: First, I would start by asking what is really on your mind at the moment. What keeps you awake?

Line Manager (LM): I'll tell you. I want to make sure that I get those darn processes done because that is how I am being evaluated. I am a loyal manager—by that I mean, a manager who produces the numbers, especially those I agree to.

HR: I would not talk that way.

[Interventionist: Fine, what would you say?]

HR: I would ask what other things are on his mind.

LM: I am bewildered. You asked me what was on my mind. I told you. Did you hear me?

HR: I think that I am trying to understand how come these ideas are on your mind. I want to understand why that thing is on your mind now.

LM: I am doubly bewildered. I thought I made it clear. I am striving to be a productive manager. So, I am going to produce according to the targets that I helped to set.

HR: What kind of targets are we talking about?

LM: You know. Produce X and Y with Z quality and do so persistently.

HR: This is sort of groping. What I am trying to understand is, given the targets, what is the disappointment at this point?

LM: The idea of disappointment is in your head, not mine. I am quite happy to do what I am doing. I am not feeling disappointed. In fact, if you would let me get on with my work, I'd be quite happy.

This series of comments is illustrative of a typical "easing-in" process. The HR professionals are seeking information that would help them be more effective. They want data on the line managers' disappointments, for example, because they believed that they could build upon pain. Their easing in ends with the comment about trying to discover any disappointments and the line managers' response that their biggest disappointment is all this HR talk.

HR (Not role playing, but commenting to the group):
"I've heard that before." (Several others nod approvingly.)

I halted the role-play and asked the group members to reflect. I said, "One of you began the session with the advice, 'Be responsive.' How responsive were you when you crafted this advice to Tom?"

HR: Not very.

[**Interventionist:** Would you please illustrate?]

HR: Maybe he was not totally listening to the line managers. I would be ready to roll up my sleeves and ask, How can I really help these guys. How can we really enter some meaningful dialogue to address their problems?

HR: And do so in a way to find out what's wrong. There has to be something wrong, or else there is not much leverage.

HR: I start with a different premise. I do not go to "sell" to anyone. I require that they come to me. It's not manipulative. It's just the way it is.

The discussion here again becomes abstract and self-referential. What does it mean, concretely, to "roll up one's sleeves," and "enter into meaningful dialogue"? But the discussion also illustrates two assumptions often held by HR professionals: first, that in order to have progress, the client must feel some pain; and second, that HR experts should not "sell" but await initiatives from the line. In both cases, it is fair to ask why.

This, in miniature, is how counterproductive cycles often get created. The Model I theories-in-use of line managers and HR experts dovetail to assure a widening gap—no matter who takes the initiative. The gap is then made worse by the inconsistency between the rhetoric around internal commitment and the examples presented, which all involved external commitment. The participants reluctantly agreed that this inconsistency did exist and that part of their job was to help line managers to see it. For the first time, several began to say that they might not understand the issues well enough to be effective.

More of the participants then began to make explicit their own sense of limitations:

HR: I am sitting here thinking, Okay. Let us admit that we do not know. Maybe we should say so and ask them to work with us to figure it out.

HR: Yes, if we can admit that what we are doing isn't working, we would then all be aligned on that. We have no idea what the hell the right "what" is, but let's figure it out together.

I paused to comment that HR experts—when they realize that they do not know as much as they should if they are to be helpful—often recommend shared dialogue in order to figure out possible answers. But how can the blind responsibly hope to lead the blind? Imagine if other types of professionals—say, accountants—were to admit that they did not know how to produce a balance sheet and then asked their clients to sit down and jointly figure out a solution.

HR: As I think about it, the most common situation that we deal with is a sense, at the gut level, that people are not authentic.

HR: Yes, people say they want to change. However, they often do not act consistently.

[**Interventionist:** How would you deal with that?]

HR: I would ask questions so that it appears that their actions aren't consistent with the commitments they made. Are you in agreement with my views or aren't you?

HR: If I see them not acting in accordance with their agreements, then I would say that sends a signal to me that they really do not agree. I can then ask, Why did you say you agree in the first place?

Others added that line managers would respond to such inquiries by saying that the "whole political structure" required them to agree even when they did not. That is how they survive. But if so, why did the HR experts not explore the inconsistencies embedded in this framing of the problem? Indeed, if line managers felt coerced by organizational defensive routines such as "politics," then why weren't these issues discussed as part of the program for getting "buy-in"? One possibility, of course, was that the HR experts were also being influenced by the same organizational defenses:

HR: It's back to the issue of internal commitment. I cannot see that it is always in people's interest to be authentic.

[**Interventionist:** Is it not fair for me to say that nowhere in the design of these programs do you advise the change professionals and the line managers to discuss this possibility? As I read the specifications, the assumption is that authenticity is always a good idea. Am I correct?]

HR: I think that it is fair to say that we believe that the overall effectiveness of our business is enhanced when people, particularly those doing the leading, act authentically. But, I believe, in the real world, it is not always in a person's best interest to be authentic. This is a huge conflict for me.

[**Interventionist:** Maybe line managers feel the same conflict. Maybe they infer that you do not see that you have the same conflict.]

HR: I am beginning to see that we—no, I—do not walk my talk *and* that I do not know how to do so.

[**Interventionist:** Is it fair to say that you were unaware of these gaps until now?]

HR: As I think about it, I would say that sometimes I was aware of the gaps, but it was when others produced them. I was not aware when I was producing them.

This is, of course, a far cry from the assertion, made at the outset of the meeting, that the responsibility for failures primarily belonged to line managers. The usual counterproductive cycle did not get into high gear because I role played the line managers as being eager to help HR experts become aware of their skilled incompetence and skilled unawareness, as well as their lack of a valid and actionable theory on which to base their programs. Nor did I push them hard on the disjunction between their espoused theory and their theory-in-use on employee commitment. Real, in-company discussions would not have been so delicate.

Many of the same problems with HR advice show up consistently in the workshop-based programs companies run to educate their executives in leadership, learning, change, and commitment. Most of these workshops, when carried out competently and even when evaluated highly by their participants, bypass the causal factors that get in the way of non-routine, transformational change.

The CEO of a very forward-looking financial organization wanted to develop a long-range program to help his institution be at the forefront of organizational learning. He asked a small task force to plan a comprehensive organizational program. The task force took a year to visit leading institutions, review the literature, interview consultants, and, in many cases, observe them delivering their programs in other organizations.

The task force recommended the creation of workshops for two thousand managers on leadership, decision making, conflict resolution, and diversity. It also suggested that the top executives take each program first. They would then evaluate the effectiveness of each program and decide whether it should be rolled out or discontinued. Both recommendations were accepted.

My colleagues and I were invited to present our program on leadership and organizational change to the top group, from whom it received positive reviews. Ahead of time, we asked each participant to do a short case write-up that included

- Identifying—in a few sentences—an important organizational problem that the individual wished to solve.
- Setting out—in a paragraph or so—the actions that the individual would take to solve the problem if there were no constraints on the kinds of actions possible.
- Splitting three or so pages into two columns and writing down, in the right-hand column, the actual conversation about these choices the individual has had (or is likely to have) with others.
- Writing out, in the left-hand column, any thoughts and feelings that were not communicated (or would not be likely to be communicated), no matter what the reason.

None of the executives in the program concluded that their case, as written, facilitated the kind of learning that each aspired to create, nor had they been aware of the gap between aspiration and performance while they were writing the cases. But they showed a high degree of interest in correcting their errors now that they had become aware of them. Meanwhile, the faculty running the program, by referring to the tape recordings, were able to show that the dialogue intended to facilitate learning *during* the workshop was effective when routine issues were discussed. But when issues were non-routine and especially when they were embarrassing or threatening, the talk was largely counterproductive.

The participants produced dialogue in their cases that, in their own retrospective evaluation, was counterproductive to the learning that they had intended to produce. But they also did so when they were trying to help other case writers correct their own unproductive actions. As a group, they were unaware of the gaps they produced while they were producing them—both in the cases and in the live dialogue. Yet they still claimed that the learning achieved by the workshops was powerful enough to justify rolling them out.

The learning they claimed to have achieved assumed a level of understanding that simply did not exist. To understand something is to be able to explain it. To explain it, it is necessary to state a causal relationship or mechanism that brings about whatever is supposed to have been understood. In other words, to be proven valid, understanding must be tested in the world of practice through the implementation of the causal claim(s) underlying it. That means the premises for any action must be made explicit, the inferences made explicit, and the conclusions put to as tough a test as possible.

All this may sound a bit obvious. Who is against productive reasoning? Who is against tough, valid tests? Almost no one—when espousing tests. But almost everyone cannot produce what he or she espouses, especially when dealing with actions that are potentially or actually embarrassing. In principle, all would agree, such gaps and inconsistencies must be closed. In practice, most people—including most HR professionals and programs—are unaware of them and their effects.

5

Concluding Observations

THE ADVICE EXAMINED SO FAR contains four characteristics that limit both its validity and its actionability. When individuals programmed with Model I theories-in-use adhere to Model I social values and comply with the requirements of organizational defensive routines, they are largely unaware of these limits. So, they actually approve the advice, value it, and feel good about it. By definition, they do not see how Model I advice, in operation, produces skilled unawareness, let alone the skilled incompetence that accompanies it. But it does. Indeed, it cannot help doing so. Here are the four main reasons why:

1. The Advice Represents Espoused Theories of Effectiveness

The advice is overwhelmingly crafted as espoused theories. Injunctions, for example, to take control, give direction, admit mistakes, be part of the solution and not the problem, truly listen, look deeper, tell it as it is, get the best out of people, and change the behavioral context do not make explicit the theories-in-use that will produce the action or result intended. Moreover, the advice does not make clear this lack of connection to action. Indeed, most of it reads as if the connection were so tangible and so obvious that there was no need to state it. But it is not, and the need is real.

If most people were programmed with Model II and regularly acted in a manner consistent with it, the positive outcomes of the advice might well appear as advertised. But they are not. Thus, whatever positive consequences emerge are, at best, temporary. As time goes by and the limits of those consequences become unmistakably clear, the advice fades away. It becomes no more than a fad to be warehoused, with many other fads, in organizational memory. My issue is not with the good intentions of the advice given or the advice givers. It goes, instead, to the accuracy of their claim, in a Model I environment, that what they offer is valid and actionable.

2. The Advice, as Crafted, Contains Evaluations and Attributions That Are Neither Tested nor Testable

Most professional advice is full of evaluations and attributions intended to help people behave more effectively. Usually, the validity of this advice is not tested, nor is the range of its applications specified. Nor, for that matter, are users told how to test it. Indeed, most advisors write as if testing were not necessary, presumably because their recommendations and promises were so obviously—and so universally—true.

Do not seek a quick fix, we are told, or blame others, or reward people for competing, or avoid personal accountability, or support the "old" pyramidal structure, or prop up the status quo. Not sometimes and in some contexts, but always and everywhere. But untested and untestable advice comes only in packages marked one size—always—fits all. There may, however, be conditions in which even actions like these enhance effectiveness or reduce ineffectiveness.

3. The Advice Is Based on Self-referential Logic That Produces Limited Knowledge about What Is Going on

Imagine a reader expressing doubt about a piece of advice and asking for proof. The answer, in most all the literature reviewed, is crafted with the use of self-referential logic: Trust me because I know what really happened or because I am sure that the status quo is counterproductive to flexibility. Far too often, advisors promise, implicitly, that their advice is valid because they know it to be so. Such promises are invalid. They are based on the same logic used to create the claim in the first place.

4. The Advice Does Not Specify Causal Processes

Advice is, basically, a claim about how to produce specified, intended consequences. Such claims, as we have seen, are difficult to implement when they do not identify the actual behaviors that are required to produce the intended consequences.

Advice is causal. If you do such and such, under defined conditions, then the intended consequences will follow. But most of the advice reviewed so far does not make explicit the causality involved. The problem is exacerbated when the advice is problematic. For example, how can defensive reactions in groups be undone by "slowing down"? What is it about slowing down that overcomes Model I theories-in-use, social values, and organizational defensive routines? How does telling people they have no choice but to get smarter create positive results or internal commitment? Exactly how does the implied causality work?

Most advice on the design and implementation of non-routine features of leadership, learning, change, and commitment is counterproductive and self-sealing because it is guided by frameworks that are based on defensive reasoning, not open and disciplined inquiry. And because it ignores the reality that most people, most of the time, hold Model I theories-in-use and Model I social values, which produce and sustain organizational defensive routines. There is nothing "soft" about Model I. It is ruthlessly programmed into people and organizations, and these programs are as hard as programs get. That is the bad news.

The good news is that people can, if they choose, learn new, Model II-compatible programs—as long as they are crafted in ways that people can actually use. The most important requirement is not to study Model II in the abstract, but to practice it, over and over, in the context of solving crucial everyday problems. That is the subject of Part II of this book.

PART II

Finding a Model that Works

6

Critiquing Advice

LET US ASSUME THAT YOU ARE INTERESTED in producing genuine organizational change. You are seeking advice about how to design and lead such changes so that they do not result in the inconsistencies, gaps, fads, and ultimately the loss of credibility that was described in Part I. How should you proceed? By carefully looking at the way the advice is crafted. In a Model I approach, individuals write or speak by advocating, evaluating, and making attributions. They craft their words in ways that include little or no illustration, inquiry, or testing. The way they make sense of their actions is to use defensive reasoning. Put simply, they believe they are correct and that their claims require no independent test; that is, they are tested, at best, by the use of what I have called self-referential logic.

In a Model II approach the individuals write or speak by advocating, evaluating, and attributing in ways that are illustrated, encourage inquiry, and are easily tested. They believe that their claims are correct, but this belief can and should be tested independently of the logic that they used to create the ideas in the first place.

I used these two models when I read the books or reported the conversations in Part I. For example, as I read someone's advice, I looked for illustrations of their views and how, if at all, the authors encouraged inquiry into and testing of their position. I made inferences about the likely use of defensive or productive reasoning by the writers or speakers. I then made my inferences subject to test. In the case of written literature, I pointed out gaps and inconsistencies plus the reasoning behind my analyses. In the case of the dialogues, I tested my inferences about gaps and inconsistencies by asking the participants to illustrate and to test. In this chapter, I would like to make my logic explicit by showing readers how they might critique the advice they receive from consultants or from popular business books.

Let me begin by critiquing a book that is among one of the most thoughtful books on change. It is called *Taking Charge of Change: 10 Principles for Managing People and Performance* (Smith 1996).*

I will then raise the kinds of questions a reader might ask, privately, about the advice offered. I will first cite the author's views. I will then suggest a series of questions, based on the theory of action perspective outlined above, that I recommend you ask yourself as you read or listen to advice. I have labeled these thoughts "private conversation."

In *Taking Charge of Change*, Smith *advises.*

The author advises. Effective leadership is based on the

---

*Smith is a management consultant who is also a co-author of another popular management book, *The Wisdom of Teams*.

courage to live the change. Living the change is the only solid ground on which to stand to lead people through transformational broad-based change.

Private thoughts. I think, and so do my colleagues, that we are capable of showing courage. But what does he mean by courage? How would we find out if we are capable of the courage he recommends?

Recall that courage, honesty, strength, and concern require radically different actions depending on whether they are being used in a Model I or Model II communication. What type does Smith recommend?

Recall also from Chapter 1 that many of the Real Change Leaders described themselves, and were described by the authors, as acting courageously. Yet they produced consequences that were counterproductive, and they did so without being aware that they were doing so.

The author advises. It requires even more courage to lead people through fundamental change.

Private thoughts. If I do not understand what is meant by courage, how would I know how to produce more of it. Smith defines fundamental change as transformational, discontinuous change and not routine change. The author does not tell me how to behave, or how to educate others to behave, in order to produce such changes.

What actual behaviors is he recommending? How do I assess how competent my colleagues and I are at leading ourselves or others?

The author advises. Taking charge and implementing broad-based change requires new skills. Gone are the days when executives can lead change through adherence to traditional hierarchical authority.

Private conversation. Apparently, Model I (unilateral authority) is out. What is he recommending? Is it consistent with Model II? The advice does not have to be consistent with Model II because there may be a more effective model. However, I am unable to specify which actual behaviors he is recommending.

The author advises. Being a champion, having a vision, emphasizing participation, using teams, encouraging new ideas are all important. In his book, Smith tells the story of Dan Holloway, a manager at Southwest Gas Electric* and Power who had championed a series of innovative change efforts. Even though Dan regularly touted the CEO's vision, delegated decision-making authority and created teams to study significant issues, Dan was not successful. He was haunted by the fact that too many of his managers lacked personal initiative and sought the security of upward approval. Dan reported that he had failed to translate the early enthusiasm from the change program into results that lasted. Too many people were letting him down (Smith, p. 105)

Private thoughts. This is reminiscent of the consequences of the change programs described in Chapter 2 that were intended to produce internal commitment yet used methods that actually encouraged only external commitment. And while the error seems familiar, the author does not describe the actual conversations that Dan crafted while he was championing, encouraging participation and the like. Without this evidence, how will my colleagues and I know whether we are making the same errors?

---

*In his book, Smith uses a technique that is common among the authors of business books. He uses real case examples, but disguises the names of both the managers and the company. Dan Holloway's story is recounted on p. 105.

Dan is making all sorts of attributions and evaluations of his colleagues. They lack initiative, the guts to make the hard decisions. He also believes that the staff at headquarters is fighting him at every turn.

Yet as Smith recounts Dan's story, it is not possible for me to know if he attempted to test the validity of his assumptions. In fact, as Smith tells the story, Dan did not engage in inquiring directly about the problems that troubled him, and Smith does not appear to recommend that Dan do the testing.

The author advises. Deal with negative behaviors in a nonjudgmental way such as by asking questions, "Have you thought about this?" or "Have you talked to so and so?"

Private thoughts. How does one know when such questions are seen as nonjudgmental and when they are seen as indirect cues as to what to do and how to act? How does one act nonjudgmentally when the basis for the action is judgmental (i.e., negative behavior of subordinates).

The author advises. "Do unto yourself what you would have others do unto themselves"

Private thoughts. How is the advice to be implemented if people are not able to act consistently with what they espouse? Moreover, how can they overcome this barrier if all parties are unaware of the inconsistencies they produce, but aware of the inconsistencies produced by others? Especially if they are likely to censor their observations and act as if they are not censoring.

The author advises. *They* (the leaders) must choose which performance results to pursue, *they* must establish broad purposes, *they* must create metrics, *they* must demand that people meet the performance demands.

Private thoughts. What specific behavior does the author believe will achieve what he advises? Isn't his advice consistent with a hierarchical top-down approach? And isn't that the very approach that he advises is out of date and ineffective?

Challenging the Change Professionals

Not all advice comes from books. Many companies hire change professionals either as consultants or in-house personnel. Let us assume for the moment that several of the senior change professionals in your company tell you that the early progress they were making has slowed. The change professionals fear that the line managers are beginning to distance themselves from the original objectives of the program: emphasizing measurable performance results, generating genuine internal commitment, and organizational learning. The change professionals contend that the line managers are increasingly focusing on "the numbers" and ignoring the human factors that everyone agreed at the outset were so important.

As the manager in this situation, you listen carefully to the change professionals, but you also realize that you need more data to truly understand the situation. So you seek a joint meeting with the CPs and line managers.

Prior to that meeting you ask the CPs to write a case. The case describes an incident that illustrates their problems and how they attempted to deal with the line managers. Also imagine that these cases are collapsed into one: a collage of the strategies that the CPs said they used. You may recall that this is the same scenario that allowed us to create Tom, the change professional whose work was previously explored in detail.*

As in that case, the next step is to meet with the CPs and use

---

*Tom, as you may recall, is symbolic of the over three hundred change professionals with whom I have worked over the last eight years.

the case as a vehicle for discussion. Let us assume that the dialogue in the case was similar to the dialogue with the CPs that was presented in Chapter 5. I would like to revisit that dialogue in order to describe the private thoughts that I had while dealing with the advice the CPs were giving to Tom. In doing so, I will attempt to model the way I would suggest that top management lead an inquiry into the competence of the CPs and the effectiveness of their designs for organizational change.

The CPs advise. CP1 advises that the key for Tom is "not to respond, but to be responsive." CP2 advises that Tom should develop "some kind of conversation, a real sense of what the survival issues are for the client." CP3 agreed and added that Tom should help the clients not feel lost.

Private thoughts. Their advice is abstract. It is crafted in terms of end results—such as be more responsive—but it does not specify what Tom might say to produce these results. Frustrated, I set out to get new information. Instead of asking the CPs what advice they would give to Tom, a solution that would only engender similar responses, I create a situation in which the change professionals use their own advice with the line managers.

To create this situation, I will role play the line managers and ask them to advise me directly—again recreating the scenario I developed in Chapter 5. Remember that it was the presumption of the change professional that in order to have progress the line manager must feel some pain. However, the line manager was clear that he felt neither pain nor disappointment. Still the change professional persisted.

It was as if the change professionals' theory-in-use was to stick to their diagnoses that the line manager was the problem, no matter what the line manager said. This increasingly upset me as I played the role of the line manager. Frustrated, I finally had to say that I did not feel understood. Indeed, I did not think that any line manager would feel understood in that situation.

The change professionals, however, believed that the manager's push-back was caused by pain and disappointment. The line manager's response was that the biggest disappointment was the CP's advice and talk. Let me recount the dialogue from Chapter 4 to illustrate.

> **CP5:** First, I would start by asking what is really on your mind at the moment. What keeps you awake?
>
> **Line Manager (LM):** I'll tell you. I want to make sure that I get those darn processes done, because that is how I am being evaluated. I am a loyal manager. (By that I mean) a manager that produces the numbers, especially those I agree to.
>
> **CP6:** I would not talk that way.
>
> [**Interventionist:** Fine, what would you say?]
>
> **CP6:** I would ask what other things are on his mind.
>
> **LM:** I am bewildered. You asked me what was on my mind. I told you. Did you hear me?
>
> **CP6:** I think that I am trying to understand how come (these ideas) are on your mind. I want to understand why is that thing on your mind now.
>
> **LM:** I am doubly bewildered. (I thought that I made it clear.) I am striving to be a productive manager. So, I am going to produce according to the targets that I helped to set.
>
> **CP6:** What kind of targets are we talking about?
>
> **LM:** You know. Produce X and Y with Z quality and do so persistently.
>
> **CP7:** This is sort of groping. What I am trying to understand

is (given the targets) what is the disappointment at this point?

LM: The idea of disappointment is in your head, not mine. I am quite happy to do what I am doing. I am not feeling disappointed. In fact, if you would let me get on with my work, I'd be quite happy.

At this point, an executive listening to this dialogue could legitimately begin to feel some concern. For example, he could begin to realize that the rhetoric of the change program was abandoned by the CPs the moment they began to experience the line manager's genuine doubt. The line manager must ask himself: To what extent does this occur in every training session and in every business session in which the CPs act as facilitators? Could this be a cause for the line managers' distancing?

As I asked the CPs to examine their own personal responsibility in creating the very problem that they identified at the outset, some began to recollect that they feared, during the early planning session, that this might happen. However, in the interest of being positive and "cooperative" they distanced themselves from the problem and covered up the distancing. The line managers also distanced themselves, but they did not cover it up.

The CPs illustrated two important problems. First, when interactions became embarrassing or threatening, they dealt with them in a Model I manner, using Model I social virtues and therefore reinforcing the existing organizational defensive routines. Second, the CPs did not have a theory that made a distinction between internal and external commitment and therefore did not have a plan to create either. The

CPs espoused internal commitment, but they acted consistently only with external commitment. This lack of focus on the causal factors produced the gaps, inconsistencies, and, eventually, the distancing from the change programs.

Rewriting the Script

Beyond critiquing the advice that others have given, I would like to illustrate how a top executive can use a theory of action perspective to help his or her immediate reports begin to reduce their counterproductive actions. In Chapter 2, I described the case of the chief information office (CIO) and his immediate reports. The latter group dealt with line mangers by creating win–lose interdepartmental relationships. The CIO attempted to help them see that they were harming themselves with little success. I should like to show how the CIO might change his private thoughts in order to reduce the interpersonal, intergroup, and organizational defenses described in the case.

The CIO must realize that he must carry on a different conversation. It should be aimed at making the issues more explicit and testing the assumptions, evaluations, and attributions related to them. When the CIO heard his subordinate say that the line managers "do not know what they want," he might carry on the following conversation with himself.

> These individuals are making evaluations of and attributions about the line's intentions without providing any data that I (or anyone else) could use to make up my own mind about the validity of their claims.

I should ask them to provide data to illustrate their claims. I have learned not to ask them "why" they believe what they do, because that will activate espoused-theory explanations that are likely to be self-serving. When the subordinates say that line managers don't know what they want, I should say, "What is it that they say or do that leads you to conclude that they do not know what they want?"

If this question is answered concretely, the CIO can make a judgment as to whether line managers are acting inappropriately. If they are, in his judgment, he can communicate these evaluations upward in order to begin to change line managers' actions.

Let us consider another example from the CIO's dialogue with his subordinates.

When the subordinates say that the line does not trust them or really care for them, the CIO could say, "Have you tested your assumptions about their views of us? If so, what did you say to the line? If not, what led you not to do so?"

If the CIO asks these questions, the subordinates might say, "Are you kidding? That would be disastrous. They would either laugh or get furious." Their response is another attribution about the line management. As such, it should be tested by the use of a logic that is different from the one used by the information technology professionals themselves. If all the CIO hears are frustrated questions, he could say something like, "When I ask you if you have tested the validity of your assertions about the line, I get another set of untested assertions. I cannot be an effective representative of our views with line management if I come to the meetings armed with untestable assertions."

If the CIO hears what he believes are incorrect or self-sealing conclusions, he could ask:

> If it is true that the users are the problem, because they do not plan and they make last-minute demands, and if it is also true that they have been doing this for years, if we get increased resources, would that not reinforce the very behavior we find frustrating?

or

> You tell me that our clients are inflexible and insensitive. That may be true. But how do you know? The only answer I get when I ask you this question is that you say they are . . . (illustrates with examples of what the subordinates have said). I would like these attributions and evaluations to be tested in ways that are independent of your reasoning. Otherwise, I could put myself in the position of being seen as an uncritical carrier of IT.

or

> I cannot go along with causal reasoning, yours or mine, when its validity is not tested independently of our views, experiences, and logic.

The CIO could also cite actions that illustrate how his subordinates may be creating the very consequences they condemn. He might say:

You stated that our customers are inflexible and insensitive (cites illustrations of such claims). You do not like this behavior, and you use it as evidence that the problems are not correctable. You may be right, but I do not hear anyone presenting a compelling argument that is also testable. Whenever I have tried to make some suggestions, the responses that I hear from you include "good luck to you" and "trust us, our users are uninfluenceable." It is difficult for me to trust your diagnosis. If you act toward the line managers the way you are acting toward me, I can see how they would become, in your eyes, uninfluenceable. But I can also see how they may come to a similar conclusion about you.

and

This leads me to another issue. You may be finding me uninfluenceable. I want to establish conversations that do not require me to distance myself from my responsibility or yours for the problems we are experiencing. I want to explore what I am saying or doing that makes me, in your eyes, uninfluenceable.

The actors should focus on reducing inconsistencies, closing gaps, and surfacing fears. For example,

INSTEAD OF	ACT AS FOLLOWS
1. Judging the players (information technology professionals, line managers, and CIO) as defensive, wrong, and unjust.	1. Request illustrations of evaluations and attributions, and craft tests of their validity.

INSTEAD OF	ACT AS FOLLOWS
2. Judging the players as naive, complainers, or crybabies.	2. Request illustrations and tests. Then inquire about how line managers acted (or would act) in response to such attempts to test. If there were no attempt to test, what was the reasoning behind such an omission?
3. Judging the players (e.g., information technology professionals) as self-centered, unfair, and unrealistic.	3. Illustrate how the gaps and inconsistencies in the actors' reasoning processes, if unrecognized, are likely to backfire.
4. Bypassing your tough evaluations about their effectiveness.	4. State your evaluations and attributions about their counterproductive actions, illustrate, and encourage testing.

Most of the advice is abstract and does not specify the theory-in-use that is required to implement it. This means that human beings will fill in the void of understanding with Model I. Some may espouse Model II, but they will be unaware of the gaps. We have seen that crafting Model II dialogue is possible, in real time, and that it is much tougher on holding people responsible for producing dialogue that will enhance double-loop learning.

7

Appraising Performance: The Dilemmas

THERE EXISTS A LONG-STANDING PARADOX in the use of performance appraisals. On the one hand, practitioners say that such appraisals are necessary to help define and ensure effective performance. On the other hand, many practitioners are also justifiably skeptical about the credibility of performance ratings—despite some quite sophisticated research on their efficacy. (See Murphy and Clevland 1995; Schuler, Farr, and Smith 1993.)

A theory of action perspective provides an explanation for this paradox and also offers a new approach to evaluating performance. Let me explain. Performance appraisals specify a series of behaviors that, if implemented as specified, will measure performance as accurately as possible. Two types of theories are used in appraising performance—the technical and the interpersonal. Technical specifications include:

1. Defining performance goals as clearly and objectively as possible.

113

2. Defining the sequence of actions required to produce the goals complete with a specified set of standards.

3. Stipulating that the goals and the actions required should be generalizable to a relevant population and comparable with the attendant proposition. For goals and actions to be generalizable they must be defined in abstract ways that are relevant to the entire population in question.

4. Translating these abstract and comprehensive concepts into dimensions that make it possible to identify the variance in the performance that is being measured. Large samples will have to be collected to help minimize the likelihood of unrecognized errors and biases and to pretest the instruments with appropriate populations.

As you can see, to form a legitimate technical rating, a fair amount of abstraction is needed. In my view, however, it is unlikely that these necessary abstractions will be comprehensive and comparable in ways that can include the richness of all the particular actions that individuals will produce in a particular case or situation. There will always be gaps to be filled, the most important of which will be evident in the actual behaviors of the rater and ratee. Most theorists have noted this fact, which brings us to the second theory of performance evaluations—the interpersonal.

Interpersonal Specifications

An interpersonal theory of performance appraisals specifies the type of interaction required to maximize the likelihood that the technical roles will be implemented correctly by both those being rated and those doing the rating. It also specifies the actions that are necessary to fill in the gaps that are not dealt with by the technical rules but are crucial in producing interpersonal relationships that encourage effective appraisal. Examples of such specifications are:

1. Illustrate the evaluations with actual behavior. Be as specific as possible.
2. Craft the illustrations in ways that minimize the likelihood that the ratee will become defensive.
3. Act in a supportive manner; exhibit concern, caring, and honesty.
4. Be open to inquiry into and confrontation of your evaluations.

As we have in previous chapters, let's now use a theory of action perspective to identify the gaps in the implementation of the technical and interpersonal requirements—things that by definition will make it difficult to carry out these tasks easily.

ADVICE	DIFFICULTIES
1. Define intended consequences and actions as clearly and objectively as possible.	1. Difficult to define for non-routine tasks, difficult to preprogram objectives, especially those that may be embarrassing or threatening. The more precise the definition, the more likely the external commitment. The more likely it will produce external commitment, the less likely that individuals at the local level will question the specifications.

ADVICE	DIFFICULTIES
2. Produce as concrete behavioral data as possible. Be objective.	2. Producing concrete behavioral data is a process of reconstructing what happened, which requires making inferences. The Model I defensive reasoning that inhibits valid inferences is rarely addressed.
3. Minimize producing defensiveness in others.	3. Model I theories-in-use produce defensiveness. Using the opposite of Model I (e.g., easing in) also produces defensiveness that is often bypassed and covered up.
4. Act in a supportive, caring manner. Be honest.	4. Model I acts of support, caring, and honesty lead to further defensiveness and self-reinforcing processes that inhibit the learning being sought.
5. Be open to inquiry; listen actively.	5. Model I leads people to be open and listen actively as long as they can win and be in control. Model I also leads them to be unaware of their skillful incompetence in being open and listening actively.
6. Use productive reasoning that encourages the above.	6. Model I encourages the use of defensive reasoning and skillful unawareness while using it.

Looking at these gaps I have come to the conclusion that implementing performance appraisals effectively by utlilizing these theories is unlikely for two reasons. The first is that the technical measurement instruments (based on productive reasoning) are crafted by the use of abstracts concepts. There is a designed gap that has to be filled in order to assess a particular individual performance. Filling the gap will become more and more dificult in jobs where tasks are non-routine and difficult to preprogram with specificity.

The second difficulty is that in order to implement the interpersonal advice, the actors should be skillful at Model II theories-in-use. Most individuals do not have such skills. Therefore, there is a strong likelihood that when difficulties and conflicts in performance activities exist, Model I will likely be activated—and this will lead to the defensive consequences already specified and illustrated.

Under these conditions Model I will dominate. Those who have greater powers are likely to prevail. Those who have less power will become appropriately submissive. They will suppress their negative feelings and act as if they are not.

These consequences are often undiscussable. The raters resist acknowledging that they are dominating because of their Model I theories-in-use. The ratees keep their responses undiscussable because they fear negative consequences. What they often overlook is that they are likely to "run silent and run deep" even when it can be established that the rater is skillful at Model II. The ratees may espouse Model II, but they find Model II social virtues of caring, concern, honesty, and integrity difficult to deal with even when those in power enable such actions (Argyris 1993, Argyris and Schön 1996).

Under these conditions, the long-standing dilemma described at the beginning of this chapter will persevere. Those working on the technical features are not addressing the difficulties because the theory-in-use embedded in their technical theories is consistent with Model I (Argyris 1980).

Those working on developing the interpersonal theories espouse Model II. However, their actions are consistent with Model I. As illustrated in Part I, they are unaware of the gap and are unaware that they are unaware.

Changing Actual Behavior

Faced with this difficult dilemma, most programs, whether they are about individual performance appraisals or group effectiveness or organizational culture, focus on changing actual behavior. There is little that is wrong with this so long as the changes required are single loop. That is, they must not require the use of a different theory-in-use. The changes that I am focusing on in this book, however, require new theories-in-use, new social virtues, and new forms of organizational dialogue. The changes are double loop. It is not possible to produce double-loop behavioral change by focusing on changing the behavior. The only way to produce double-loop behavioral change is to introduce new theories-in-use as Model II.

If it is true that most human beings use Model I, then if the behavioral change required is consistent with, and remains within, the limits of Model I, it should not be too difficult to change the behavior because the individuals have the appropriate theory-in-use. The difficulties arise when the changes require a theory-in-use that they do not hold. As we have seen, all the change programs, be they individual, group, or organizational culture, espouse Model II theories-in-use and social virtues.

Such programs will not be effective unless the individuals become aware of how skillfully unaware they are of their defensive reasoning and the consequences that they produce. Finally, the change programs must introduce learning opportunities to become skillful at Model II and productive reasoning. As we have seen in Part I, none of the programs focused on producing these requirements.

I should like to illustrate the difficulties that arise when the focus is on changing behavior and the intention of the change program is to produce double-loop change. Let's assume that an individual is observed as controlling unilaterally what is said or cutting off individuals in the middle of making their point. Acting unilaterally and cutting people off are evaluated as having a negative impact on open dialogue and effective problem solving. It follows that the unilateral and cutting-off behavior should be reduced.

How? By making a deliberate effort not to cut people off. The way to implement this advice is through actual "practice" in workshops and eventually in everyday problem-solving meetings. "Practice" means that individuals strive to produce the new behavior. It also means that they learn to reflect on the impact of their behavior in order to detect and correct errors. This, in turn, requires the help of others.

But how do individuals produce the new behavior? Only by having a design that is warehouseable in and retrievable from the human mind—a theory-in-use. If the individuals' theories-in-use are Model I, then the only behavior that they will be able to produce is more of the unilateral behavior. The exception is if they are able to suppress the use of the Model I the-ory-in-use. One way to suppress the Model I theory-in-use is to act in the opposite manner.

Recall that Model II is not the opposite of Model I. The opposite of Model I is to suppress the unilateral behavior. Indi-viduals who are able to suppress their Model I behavior are able to do so because the skill that is required is essentially to keep quiet and "be patient." In other words, if individuals sup-press Model I action, the expectation is that the unilaterally controlling individuals may see that the others do blossom and new ideas are generated. Such reactions, in turn, ideally lead them to continue suppressing Model I.

This means that the Model I theories-in-use are not changed, they are simply suppressed. It also means that it is highly likely that the suppression will be stopped the moment the individuals feel that things are getting out of hand and they could lose control. At that moment, they will return to Model I, in order to retain control.

Consider, for example, a meeting that I attended with three senior partners who, in their words, had been "Coveyised." The three evaluated the educational experience positively. One said that it helped him to be patient with a manager who had difficulty in taking initiative. He strove to deal with the manager by being patient and positive.

I asked him to illustrate what he typically said to that man-ager. The answer was, in effect, to encourage the manager. "I know you can do it," or "Give it a try," or "I'll be glad to help you with any ideas that you bring up." All this is consistent with Covey advice to be positive.

I then took the role of the "passive" subordinate and pro-duced fancy footwork to cover myself. The partner, after a few minutes said, "Yes, he says stuff like that. After a while I get frustrated and if it lasts long enough, I become infuriated." He quickly added that he does his best not to act infuriated and continue to be as positive as he could be.

The senior partner struggled not to make the passive subordinate defensive. He produced his sense of compassion and concern by largely suppressing his feelings of frustration and infuriation. All this is consistent with Model I theories-in-use and Model I social virtues.

The senior partner then asked me how I would deal with such a subordinate. In a role-playing exercise, the senior partner acted as the subordinate and produced the predictable fancy footwork. Playing the role of the senior partner (SP), I then said to "Joe," the passive leader in question:

> **SP:** Joe, I am trying to be of help. One of my intentions is to help you take on more initiative and be more proactive.
> **Joe:** Yes, I hear that.
> **SP:** Let me review the bidding. When I say (such and such) you respond (such and such). I then respond and you said such and such. (illustrates). "I have reached the end of my know-how. If you think that I have not been acting helpfully, please say so and illustrate what would have been more helpful. Otherwise, in all honesty, I will conclude that I cannot be of help. You may wish to seek help elsewhere. Fine, but the final test is in our relationship. It is unlikely that I will be able to evaluate you positively in the future.

The senior partner responded that what I said made sense. He also said that he thought of saying something like it, but did not because doing so would not be seen as positive and supportive. My response was to review the Model II meanings of support and show how my words were consistent with such meanings.

Performance Management by the Book

Let's consider another, similiar example, this time from a book called *Reengineering Performance Management,* by Weiss and Hartle (1997). The authors advise that good feedback is specific rather than general; it is recent; it is descriptive; it is not judgmental; it stands alone; and it is given as part of a two-way discussion. The authors point out that this advice is easier to implement when criteria for effective performance are clear and unambiguous (e.g., answer the telephone before the third ring, submit weekly expense reports on time). This advice focuses on behavior that can be implemented without having to learn new theories-in-use.

The problem with the advice arises when the behavior required requires a theory-in-use that the actors do not have. That is why they must advise the raters to focus on behavior that can be changed. The only way that this advice is implementable is if the individuals already have the proper theory-in-use. But, if they did, the developmental changes would be routine, not double loop.

Imagine using this type of advice to help Covey himself. It would not get at the fact that his theory-in-use is Model I and the opposite of Model I. How would this advice help Tom? How does it deal with the defensive reasoning used by Tom as illustrated by his left-hand columns?

How would the advice help the two dozen CPs advising Tom? For two hours I gave relevant feedback that would, if taken, have led to the results that they were advising Tom to produce. As the transcript shows, they did not recognize the feedback as positive. Their fancy footwork was to blame the managers. It took several hours of persistence on my part before they began to examine their personal responsibility. But, even after they did, and even after they could verbalize how they might have behaved, they were unable to do so because the only theory-in-use they had was Model I or its corollary, the opposite to Model I.

Moreover, some, on reflection, saw my actions toward them as " a bit too confronting" and "tough," to quote two participants. These reactions often occur when the facilitator is acting consistently with Model II social virtues (Argyris 1982, 1990a; Argyris, Putnam, and Smith 1985, Argyris and Schön, 1996).

Another limitation can be illustrated by the advice the authors give a manager when the person he or she is attempting to coach does not seem coachable. The manager is advised to ask:

1. What is preventing the individual from accepting feedback without being defensive?
2. What is keeping this person from sharing information with me?
3. What does my tone or the words I'm using convey? The manager is also asked to probe for possible fears that the individual has and examine how to reduce those fears.

The frame from which these questions are derived assumes that the responsibility for the resistance lies in the individual receiving the feedback and assumes that the resistance is probably due to fear. All this may be true. But, as I have illustrated, it could be that the cause is not so much fear or resistance. Instead, the individual, guided by Model I theories-in-use and Model I social virtues, may actually believe that he or she is acting cooperatively.

Such a line of inquiry is precisely the kind that got the CPs in trouble because it allows the coaches to ignore their theory-in-use and their degree of skilled incompetence and skilled unawareness.

Finally, the authors tell us the story of Bridget. As a result of some "360-degree" feedback, she learns that she is high on being authoritative. She is medium on coercive, democratic, and coaching. Bridget, on the other hand, viewed herself as medium/high on affiliate, democratic, and coaching, medium on authoritative and low on coercive.

The authors conclude that this combination of styles creates a workplace climate that is very friendly but lacking in clear direction. Bridget, the authors advise, needs to close these gaps. She must improve two styles: authoritative and coaching. How is Bridget to implement this advice? Bridget should jointly set stretching yet realistic objectives, focus on continuous improvement, identify actions needed to overcome potential/actual obstacles to meeting objectives, communicate standards expected, and model them in her performance. She should not tolerate mediocrity or lower standards.

How does she do this? Her theory-in-use is the opposite of Model I. How are these styles altered? Why is she not asked to examine how come she was unaware of the discrepancy between her views of herself and those of her immediate reports? How do we know that the subordinates' evaluations are not systematically biased by their own theories-in-use and social virtues? Why do the authors not advise Bridget, and her immediate reports, to examine these questions before she or anyone else changes their behavior? Moreover, what will happen if there is such an inquiry? Will not the Model I theories-in-use, fancy footwork kick in? If not, there is nothing in the advice the authors propose that will prevent it from occurring. If so, how will they deal with the self-fueling anti-learning consequences?

Finally, let us examine the advice given for dealing with resistance to change (Fitzgerald and Kirby 1997). The authors advise that the rater should first decide what she wants the person to do. Then consider what would cause the rater to resist and determine what actions to take for addressing the concerns the rater has attributed. All this advice is consistent with Model I (e.g., rater decides what ratee should do, rater makes attributions about causes of resistance, rater acts on these attributions). Next, the rater should consider possible objections that the ratee may have and be prepared to respond. But how should the rater craft the responses? What would be the actual conversation? The author is mute on such questions.

Finally, in order to reduce causes of resistance to the rater's recommendations, the authors recommend that informal discussions be held to review the reasons for the feedback process; that the raters encourage participation whenever possible; that they present plans as tentative and solicit advice and suggestions; and that they give people control over their feedback. What is not discussed is how the conversations should be crafted; what actions are required for encouraging participation when the ratee is resisting, what the likelihood is that resisting ratees would take unfair advantage of the tentativeness, and finally, how to give the ratees control over their feedback when the ratees may be taking control by resisting the feedback.

8

Evaluating Group Performance

NOW, AS IN PREVIOUS CHAPTERS, I would like to demonstrate how a Model II type of inquiry can be used to evaluate the performance of a group. The vice president in charge of a consulting team asked the five members to meet with him to reflect on their effectiveness as a team and on the service provided to the client. He was interested in learning why a team of two very competent consultants and three managers, all of whom had successfully completed a similar project in another part of the client organization, did not produce the high-quality work expected by the firm and the client. The vice president believed that self-reflection could strengthen the capacity of the consulting firm, through its professionals, to detect and correct its errors.

First, I will present excerpts from the tape-recorded conversation. Next, I explore step-by-step the reasoning the participants must have gone through to produce the conversation. Then I examine the causal theories involved in the conversations. Finally, I analyze the reasoning processes the players used when they acted on their diagnosis. As we will see, the primary action was a massive cover-up of which the actors were unaware at the time but saw clearly when they reflected on their actions.

> **Vice president:** One reason I called this meeting is because I don't understand [why we did not produce as good a product for the client as we could have]. This is probably as good a case team as can be put together. The people are good, the level of experience is good (for the most part), the client liked and respected us, our client skills are quite good [and finally, we had done a similar study for the client in another location].

The officer then asked the case team to be candid.

> **Vice president:** I'll talk last because I do not want to bias what others say. [I'll give my report and I promise to be candid]. And I would say that we are all strong enough and big enough around here that we should be straightforward in our evaluations. I don't think that we gain anything by not being straightforward about all our roles, including officers as well as managers.

The vice president then asked the others to give their views.

> **Manager 1:** I think we had a lot of chiefs and no Indians. Second, we never made explicit our internal [case team] organization. As a result of changing [client] conditions, redefinition of the case, we ended up not being clear, and

the changes over time caused a lot of resentment and were counterproductive.

Manager 2: Everybody had his individual piece, but people did not know what the others were doing.

Manager 1: And finally, there was some backbiting as well. Also, the vice president had to change his time commitment [in midstream], and [Manager 3] was to compensate for his time. But I do not believe that was made explicit.

Consultant 1: I agree. We went into the field intensively, and once in the field, it was kind of irretrievable. [Later on, when new issues surfaced, we could not] go back to the field in a cost-effective way. So I think we could have done more thinking before we went into the field.

Manager 2: Also, since the order was to go out to do the market interviews, we had little time to interact as a case team. Nobody was really coordinating the case from a holistic point of view. [Provides detailed example.] The whole thing was basically out of control.

Interventionist: When did you sense that the project was out of control?

Manager 2: Between the start of the project and the first presentation. [Another thing], we [rarely] met as a case team without the client so that we could integrate our work. It was always more of a "show-and-tell" presentation. We never had a normal case team meeting without the client and without the "show and tell."

Manager 1: We also needed you [the vice president] during the first presentation to the client. Just the fact that you weren't there in a situation where we were getting nitpicked to death. . . . I don't think any of us, and many of us tried, could stop [the nitpicking]. I think maybe you could have. I don't know why we couldn't stop [it]. I remember sitting there saying, "My God, we just killed ourselves for a week and I'm watching this presentation just get torn to hell for nonsensical reasons."

[**Interventionist:** What could the vice president have done that none of you could have done?]

Consultant: Acted vice presidential!

Manager 1: "Acted vice presidential" is probably the perfect answer. It climaxed for me during [Consultant 2's] presentation. It wasn't one of his greatest, and it wasn't particularly bad. . . . The message didn't come through and they were nitpicking us on numbers that were their own creation. . . .

I remember sitting in that meeting and saying (to myself), "You have three choices. You can keep your mouth shut, and that wouldn't work. You can try to contribute when [the client is] getting off the point. Or you can try and stand up and say, "Listen, you turkeys, you're being idiots. Stop the nonsense. Here is our message." And I did not have the guts to do that.

Manager 2: Yes, that would have helped.

Manager 1: Which you [points to the vice president] would have done as a matter of course.

[**Interventionist:** What would you have expected the vice president to say?]

Manager 1: [Roughly, he would say], "Today's session is an interim presentation. We are here to update you as to our progress. We also want to make sure that we're not getting totally off the track. I think the level of detail that you people are trying to explore is getting us off the track." Then he would give some examples and literally bring the meeting to a halt until that issue was resolved.

[**Interventionist:** And you do not think anyone on this team would have said that with credibility?]

Manager 1: I think [Manager 3] could try.

Consultant 1: I heard [another officer] once say to the clients in a meeting, "It doesn't matter what the number is. The point is, your performance in that area is lousy. It doesn't matter if it is 80 percent or 70 percent lousy. Once you're below 95 percent, it is awful. All right?" And he just totally shut the client up, and [the client's] boss kept a quiet approval. He can probably get away with it because officers have equal level relationships with the client. And none of us would dare do it, no matter how senior we are. Or even if we did, it wouldn't come off the same.

Manager 3: [I tried several times to do something like Consultant I describes], but there were so many levels of the client organization present—the [client] was sitting there having a field day. It was a zoo. I would like to put the mantle on you [vice president]—and you probably could have pulled it off, but it was a difficult situation. It was difficult in a curious way because it wasn't particularly rancorous, it was just nit-picking.

Manager 2: [Returns to the issue that] we never had a chance among ourselves to say what the hell are we trying to accomplish? What are the issues, anyway?

[To another case team member]: I remember you said [such and such], and I sat there and I didn't even know what that meant. You made it sound important, but I didn't know what that meant.

Consultant 2: [Since there was a lack of coordination], I
didn't know how to really pitch in and take the burden off
[someone], because I didn't understand what we were
doing as a whole, but I never said so. And everyone was
working madly . . . and the harder people work, the more
frantic it is . . . the harder it is to tell anyone to do something
or to give someone something to do.

Manager 3: I think I agree with most of what has been said.
As I hear this, I have learned that probably I should have
been a little more forceful [about the lack of coordination
and who is the leader]. It was difficult to do so because I did
not have the vice presidential imprint so that I could say,
"Now look, I want you guys to do this." And so I was listening to [the case team members] in a soundingboard sense
rather than trying to take control. . . . Maybe that was a
mistake.

I think the client was not easy [during the first presenta-
tion]. To this day, I haven't figured out whether we were
talking at one level and hearing something back at a different
level, or what the heck was going on. As a result, [we created our own explanation. We decided] that they were
crazy, not us, and you know, don't worry, we'll come around
in the final analysis and we'll give them value for the money.

Finally [because we had done this case before], there was
an incredible fixation to come up with something that was
different. And I think you [Manager 2] created a segment out
of whole cloth just to try to satisfy yourself that in fact you
had added something new and creative. Because I think that
we were all disappointed . . . you know, this is a pretty bor-
ing business. I mean, there was nothing new under the sun.

This was not my favorite assignment. Oh, yes, and, finally, I think in the final analysis we came up against a client to whom we were saying things that the client did not want to hear (illustrates).

Vice president: OK, let me add a few more points. Our senior client contact, Jones, had just been made head of another outlet. They did not want their operation to report to the United States The old story of the United States over-taking. Hence, Jones was reluctant to force us down the throats of the client organization. That was why he asked for the most senior case team he could have so there would be lots of interaction with the clients. One reason we went into the market early was that Jones believed that his organiza-tion did not know what they were doing in the market. . . .

We have learned that it is difficult to have three levels of clients who all think they are clients. On the other hand, I do not think that we coped with it. We knew about this problem, and I do not think any of us, me especially, did a particularly good job. . . .

The case team meeting in May left me with the impres-sion that you hadn't learned a damn thing. And not only that, you focused so explicitly on the businesses that they were in and so little on the peripheral sides of the business that [our presentation] would have been a disaster.

That is why I made the changes [that you described]. I said to myself that we can't show something that ignores half of the other guy's business.

And I think one of the major lessons here is that never through the whole case, until the end, did I feel that I could turn to any one of you for a holistic view of what the client's products were. I felt that each of you knew your own little piece and you were all going to do your own little piece as well as you could do it, without getting your ass in gear.

Not only that, but each of you specifically thought the other guy was not doing his job. There were people saying, "[Manager 2] didn't do his job," and [Consultant 1] said, "Did you see [Consultant 2 is] going to get credit for what [Manager 1] did?" [and I could give more examples].

And so I had no one coming to my office and saying, "I think, in fact, we're not facing the real issue." I didn't have a single guy come in and do that. Not once in the whole study did somebody come in and say, "I think we're looking at this wrong." [Manager 3] and I did do that toward the end, which is why we finally wrote the report ourselves.

And look, I was guilty too, because I just left the scene, so I can't claim that I'm a great help.

We each had our own little piece, and we came in here and showed it, and they [the client] came in the next day and said it was terrible. They did it at every single meeting after that. [Manager 3] and I could fend them off [and so we privately] reorganized the presentation so that it covered more of the whole.

I think that the reason the first meeting went bad was because we had bad stuff [data and analysis]. I do not think that it went bad because I was not there. I don't think if I had been there I could have done what many of you said. I'm very glad I wasn't there, because I would have had to stand up and defend you guys, and it was probably bad stuff. . . .

For example, we produced the wrong forecast, and that is serious. I do think that they picked the hell out of us, but they would have tried that with me there. It would have taken some amount of chutzpah to get us through the meeting, no matter what. After that, I'm sure we made a mistake in having them there for the briefing. That was a terrible mistake. [However, it is working in another client situation because we are maintaining intimate ongoing contacts with them, something we did not do in this case.] . . .

If I were to state the generic problem, I think the Indians/chiefs is the real one. That's important because if we are to be successful, we will have to have a lot of Indians. [In the future], we've got to sell more million dollar-at-a-whack cases, which means more cases like this one down the road. That's the way we've got to go.

We've got to learn to work together, each carrying the weight of our salary in our billing range. And that means we need to identify, keep the whole in place, and then be able to approach each other when the work isn't good enough.

[We also must] approach the person who is leading [the project] and say, "I don't think that we're addressing the big issues here"—instead of each guy looking like "All I have to do is just make sure I don't get my ass in a sling and I'm billable and then I'll be doing good work."

Manager 3: The vice president gave me a lot of free rein, short of saying explicitly . . . you know, he said to me, "I'm going to be busy at another case, so I'm going to rely on you." I think that put me in a difficult position because that statement was never made explicit to anybody else. Nor did I make the statement any more emphatically to anybody else than you made it to me.

Maybe an error was that I didn't begin to behave in more of a general/admiral kind of fashion. I found it difficult to have two fellow managers on the case. It got difficult to go to you and say, "Look, damn it, go do that." In my experience around here, two reactions can ensue from that approach. One is "Go screw yourself [Manager 3]." The other is "That's terrific, [Manager 3]"—and then all of a sudden it starts coming back through the grapevine [that the person] was really upset.

Let me ask, is there anything that I did that dissuaded you from coming in and telling me, "This thing is going wrong?"

Unidentifiable speaker: I didn't see much of you.

Manager 2: I guess there is really no good answer. We should have come to you. I know that I didn't say a peep, and I don't think that I heard much of a peep from anybody else other than the kind, you know, on the airplane. The question was asked, "Why are we doing this?" but nobody ever said, "Maybe we should stop right now and do something else." [Several persons say yes.]

Consultant 1: But [to return to your question], I didn't get the feeling that if I said something to you about it . . . things would change that much.

Manager 3: What do you mean by that?

Consultant 1: If I have a feeling that we are poorly organized but do not have real hard data or facts, how is talking about it going to change what you are doing?

Manager 3: What do you mean by that?

Consultant 1: If I have a feeling that we are poorly organized but do not have real hard data or facts, how is talking about it going to change what you are doing?

I saw you [and others] busy. You were running around. I figured the last thing you're going to have time to do is sit down and spend a lot of time trying to figure out if some-thing's wrong when the only reason I'm saying it is because I do not see much interaction going on.

The interventionist reported that Jones, the client, had said he was disappointed with the case team's performance and that he blamed the vice president for it. Jones felt that a case team was as good as its vice president and this one, he said, was superb. The problem, as he saw it, was that the vice president had become overcommitted. Jones had expected that the vice president would pull together a case team report that was technically good, understandable, and communicable and that he would have the team working cooperatively with the client's inner group. The interventionist gave excerpts from Jones's conversation: "Regarding the vice president, he is very bright. But, more important, he can come alive and make something complex become clear. It makes it possible for us to understand him and also to question him. Without the vice president, I wouldn't buy this. I don't think that I could have sold this case to the group."

Factors that Inhibited Performance

As we have just seen, the case team members identified the following causal factors inhibiting their performance:

1. There were too many chiefs and not enough Indians. Chiefs like to manage, and there was no one to be man-aged.
2. Not enough time was set aside at the outset of the pro-ject to think it through.

3. The consultants did their own work in ignorance of what others were doing and did not take the initiative to find out what the others were doing. They saw themselves as individual contributors rather than team members.
4. Team meetings should have been held without the clients present.
5. Some backbiting occurred among consultants.
6. The vice president withdrew from active management and no one filled the vacuum.
7. The manager who was the logical successor did not take adequate initiative to manage the case team.
8. The team lacked a vice president who could "act vice presidential" at the first client presentation to stop the client's nit-picking.
9. Managers felt helpless in dealing with the nitpicking client and suppressed their frustration. The client reps escalated their counterproductive activities, infuriating the team members. The meeting was a disaster.
10. Parts of the case were so routine that some members overinvested time and energy just to come up with something different.

Reasoning Processes Involved in Inferring These Inhibiting Factors

The factors just listed are inferences made by the team members about what caused the team's below par performance. The partial and complete transcripts show that all the participants confirmed the relevance of each factor. Factors 1, 2, 3, 4, and 6 were identified as important, with the first one, "Too many chiefs and not enough Indians," being the key factor.

The existence of a strong consensus among the members is not adequate evidence that these were the only causal factors. The team members might unknowingly be ignoring other important factors. Indeed, I hope to show that they were.

The next step in the analysis is to answer this question: What were the reasoning processes used to arrive at the consensus? One objective of the meeting was for each member to state what he believed were the causal factors that produced the less than desired performance—that is, to make a diagnosis. Each person gave his views, illustrating them whenever possible by sifting through his own experiences as well as he could recollect them. These conclusions become the basis for our analysis. For example:

PARTICIPANTS' COMMENTS	INFERENCE ABOUT WHAT TEAM MEMBERS EXPERIENCED
Nobody was really coordinating the case from a holistic point of view.	Individuals recognized coordination problems but did not discuss them or take corrective action.
I remember you said . . . and I sat there and I didn't even know what that meant.	Members were reluctant to discuss issues if it meant stepping on each other's toes.
I didn't really know how to pitch in . . . because I didn't understand what we were doing as a whole, but I never said so.	The team members realized early on that they could produce a better product if there were greater clarity about objectives early in the case.

PARTICIPANTS' COMMENTS	INFERENCE ABOUT WHAT TEAM MEMBERS EXPERIENCED
We went into the field intensively [too early]. . . . We could have done more thinking [about the case] before we went into the field. We rarely met . . . without the client so that we could integrate our work. It was always more of a "show-and-tell" presentation. We never had a normal case team meeting without the client. . . .	Consultants experienced difficulty in case team meetings because client representatives were present.
The whole thing was basically out of control. . . . I did not have the vice presidential imprint so that I could say, "Now, look, I want you guys to do this."	Once the vice president withdrew, the manager who was the logical choice for second-in-command did not take charge.

The team members' experiences described in the right-hand column became the premises for the next step in the reasoning process. For example:

TEAM MEMBERS REPORTED	*THEY THEREFORE CONCLUDED*
The managers and consultants recognized the coordination problems as they occurred, but they neither discussed them nor took corrective action. It seemed as if the managers and (perhaps less so) the consultants did not wish to step on each other's toes.	Too many chiefs, not enough Indians.
It was soon obvious that the experience of a similar case was not an adequate guide. Team members felt they would have produced a better product if objectives had been clearer at the outset. . . .	Team leadership did not take time to examine the assumptions and directions of the case because they did not see these matters as important. . . .
Consultants experienced difficulty in several case team meetings because client representatives were present.	Some team meetings should have been held without clients, but team leadership did not schedule such meetings.
Once the vice president withdrew, the manager who was the logical choice for second-in-command did not take charge.	Manager did not wish, or did not feel free to take charge.

TEAM MEMBERS REPORTED	THEY THEREFORE CONCLUDED
Case team members felt helpless to control client's nitpicking during early sessions.	Vice president could have blunted counterproductive behavior of client.

Responsibility for the Causal Factors

Under these reasoning processes is a second, deeper level of causal factors. The team members place responsibility for the first-level factors on gaps in judgment, inherent limitations of participants, and unforeseen events. For example:

IF	THEN
Not enough time was allocated during the early stages to think the case through.	The responsibility was the officer's and we (managers and consultants) had better not question his judgment. He is highly skilled; therefore, he will realize when the case is not progressing and blow the whistle, and he knows how to deal with difficult clients.
There were too many chiefs and not enough Indians;	The managers did not act as if they had the capacity simultaneously to be managers and effective case team members.

Each participant acted as an individual contributor;	Good team members need only make their individual contributions. The vice president's responsibility is to generate and maintain effective team interdependence.
We had too many meetings with the clients;	The vice president must have known what he was doing by inviting the client to our meetings; we had better acquiesce.
The team lacked a vice president who could act vice presidential.	The vice president was responsible for creating a gap that could not be filled by others.

These second-level factors fall into three categories:

1. *Gaps in judgment.* For example, the vice president erred in not allocating more time to early case team meetings and in inviting clients to meetings.
2. *Self-imposed limitations in members' actions.* For example, Manager 3 did not exercise leadership so no one integrated the individual contributions into a whole until the end.
3. *Unforeseen actions become counterproductive to the team's effectiveness.* An example is the vice president's withdrawal.

We now see that we have two levels of factors operating to cause the poor team performance. The first and more manifest factors—that is, those close to the surface—are the ones the case team identified. The second and more latent factors—those below the surface—are those inferred from the reasoning processes that led to the first factors.

The two levels of factors give significantly different targets for change. Moreover, if the second level causes the first, then correction of the first level is no guarantee that the second will not continue to exist to create difficulties in another situation. To complicate matters, the first-level factors can be used to avoid examining the second-level factors. Therefore, there must be a tacit consensus, or groupthink, operating among the team members of which they are unaware. What could cause their tacit consensus, and why are they unaware?

Primary Recommendation

To answer these questions, let us turn to the primary recommendation made by the case team members. The overwhelming consensus was for a chief who could be tough and forthright and exhibit take-charge leadership. This consensus continued even after the team members read a draft of the transcript. For example, the vice president said, "Looking backwards in order to deal with the future, I think that I would get mad at these guys sooner," and "I could have endorsed [Manager 3] more directly, but he is a senior and respected manager [and so] I did not believe that he needed the mantle."

Their target, therefore, is to create a clear chain of command under someone who is able to coordinate and give orders and to whom the team members can communicate their views. Unilateral power in the hands of a case team leader is the recommended solution.

This recommendation, however, has limited effectiveness. Holding meetings to set the objectives of the case and holding meetings without the client present could not be achieved solely by the appointment of a chief. The major requirement is that the chief sense, and/or the team members tell him, that such action is necessary.

The vice president might have been willing to take such action if he had been so advised by the case team members, although he expressed doubts about the advisability of excluding clients. One could add further reservations about the team's recommendation: appointing a chief may not solve the problem if the chief makes errors but is not particularly confrontable. His effectiveness could be seriously compromised in a team in which the trust level is low. Appointing a chief, therefore, is no guarantee that problems will be solved in a way so they remain solved.

A chief does assure, however, that team members do not have to focus on the errors in their own actions and reasoning processes. For example, the team members could have communicated upward information about the factors that were harming the team's effectiveness; they could have explored the reasoning processes that led them to place the responsibility elsewhere; they could have explored the implications of their lack of initiative. They could have done these and more, but they did not because in their minds their actions were not errors and their reasoning was not faulty. They sincerely believed that what they did was in the interest of the organization. The analysis that follows will partially support this belief. Hence, we have a paradox: actions that are in support of the organization necessarily also harm it. But how was this paradox created? Who is responsible for such conditions?

Several individual and organizational factors combine to cause the problem. The professionals have developed a strategy to protect themselves from pressure and from feelings of failure, a strategy that distances them from any responsibility for the internal system of the organization. For example:

TEAM MEMBERS' ACTIONS	*FEATURES OF DISTANCING*
They identified factors that inhibited the team's effectiveness and chose to act as if they did not see them and to hide the act of hiding. Thus, there was a cover-up and a cover-up of the cover-up.	Individuals distanced themselves from their personal causal responsibility for both the coverup and the coverup of the coverup.
They chose not to go public with the cover-up when the vice president requested that they do so in the interests of individual and organizational learning.	Team members distanced themselves from cover-up responsibility by holding the vice president responsible for breaking the cover.
They also chose not to go public about the cover-up of their cover-up.	And they distanced themselves from any responsibility for continuing the cover-up of their cover-up.

They chose to focus on the manifest (surface) factors and continued to suppress the latent (depth) factors.	Members distanced themselves from their decision to hide the latent factors and to focus on the causal, manifest factors.
The surface factors could be altered by creating organizational rules that would reduce each team's effectiveness.	They also chose to hide the personal responsibility for the latent factors.

The professionals report a high degree of pressure and tension related to client relationships. They accept these pressures as legitimate, but there is a limit to how much pressure they can absorb. Hence, they habitually distance themselves from what they call "unnecessary and illegitimate pressures." Issues related to administration are viewed as unnecessary and illegitimate in the sense that they take too much time or get mired in long, tedious meetings. This kind of thinking evolves from the same reasoning processes the team members used in this case.

What led the vice president to make errors in judgment? One reason was that he had taken on too many assignments and was absent from meetings more than he should have been. But no one told the vice president that the team needed him or why. Perhaps team members were afraid to communicate upward, being apprehensive about his reaction. (Although such apprehension happened not to be a problem in this situation. I learned from subordinates that they would be careful in communicating upward with certain officers. Such information runs counter to the advice that a chief in unilateral control will solve the problem.) However, this vice president is one of the officers most concerned about human relationships. Indeed, the very act of holding such a meeting and opening up his own actions to inquiry illustrates his interest in personal and organizational learning.

The Next Steps

The next step was for the individuals to invent new solutions. These solutions included developing new rules about effective member behaviors and group norms to support the new behaviors. Once these were agreed on, the members experimented with producing the actual conversation. For example:

1. **Solution:** If you believe that coordination problems exist, say so, and encourage testing of the attribution. **Production:** I should like to test an attribution about our group action. [From such and such examples - illustrate with concrete conversation], I infer that we have a coordination problem. Do others of you recollect the conversation? Would they lead you to reach the same or different conclusions?
2. **Solution:** If you do not examine the assumptions, test out the likely effectiveness of not doing so with others. **Production:** Here are two assumptions that I believe we are making and that, at least, are not discussing, because I believe they are not important. Do others agree that we are making these assumptions and that they are not important?

3. **Solution:** If you see a cover-up and a cover-up of the cover-up, test the attribution and help to produce new actions.

   Production: I should like to test an attribution about our group's process. [From these conversations cites them], I infer that we are hiding ideas about our lack of effectiveness and that we are not discussing the substance or the cover-up. What are your reactions?

The Methodology Used by the Interventionist

During the session, I intervened very little. The objective was to have the participants produce as much conversation as possible that illustrated their views of what happened during the second relationship. After nearly two hours of dialogue, I began to intervene. My interventions were guided by Model II. Because they are similar to the ones described in the Tom case, I will not repeat them.

I would like to focus on a different aspect of the methodology. How would I go about organizing and making sense of the conversations (from the tape recordings)? How would I feedback this result so that it would help the consultants learn how to diagnose and map their own diagnostic session as well as those with clients?

The structure of the report would be similar to the structure of the diagnosis just described.

1. Identify the causal factors that the team members cited as inhibiting their effectiveness. Do so by using their language (test the validity of this description with the team members).

2. Identify the reasoning process that the team members used to arrive at the inhibiting factors. Try to surface inferences about group effectiveness that were embedded in the comments and were not made explicit by the participants. For example, from the comment, "Nobody was really coordinating the case," I inferred that the individuals recognized the existence of coordinating problems but did not discuss them.

3. Identify the causes stated by the group members to explain what led them to act as they did. For example, from the diagnosis that the coordination problems existed but were not discussed, the cause was, as the group members saw it, too many chiefs and not enough Indians.

4. Identify who was responsible for their counterproductive actions. For example, they held the officer responsible *and* they held themselves responsible for not questioning his actions.

5. The analysis points to two levels of factors causing poor team performance. The first set was closer to the surface. The second set was below the surface.

6. Identify the actions acquired to alter both sets of factors.

7. Point out the self-protective actions on the part of all concerned. For example, individuals distanced themselves from their causal responsibility for the cover-up and the cover-up of the cover-up.

8. Develop group norms that encourage this kind of diagnosis whenever the group seems to be getting into trouble or during scheduled meetings to reflect on the group's performance.

Experience with this kind of diagnosis will help to identify skilled incompetence and unawareness, defensive reasoning, and counterproductive group learning processes and to design Model II productive reasoning to reduce the counterproductive cycles produced by individuals and by the group.

The Influence of Organizational Defensive Routines on Effective Performance

The Model I theories-in-use and social virtues are not the only major causes of the poor credibility of performance appraisals. All performance appraisals occur in an organizational context. This context is dominated by organizational defensive routines that make double-loop learning less likely. They also provide cultural support for this gap—indeed, for not even seeing the gap.

I should like to illustrate by drawing on my recent experience with several large organizational programs in which I had been asked to assist in evaluating these change programs. The illustrations of Tom and the encounters with the change professionals (Part I) were taken from these experiences. In all the examples that I reviewed, the change programs began with top management asserting that competitiveness is key in a global environment. Top management then called for fundamental changes such as, "Our company's future will depend, in no small measure, on our ability to adapt." Or "Organizational learning is key." And "It is time that we review the risk-averse culture that we have produced." And, finally, "We must confront the tough issues squarely and honestly."

The next step was the appointment of a team of managers

from several levels in the organization. The managers were selected because they were excellent performers and were seen as "highfliers." These teams worked diligently. They took top management's rhetoric about being tough and forthright seriously. For example, one team advised that the new values call for:

LESS	MORE
Responding to instructions	Proposing action
Pleasing the boss	Accountability
Accepting under-performance	Security via personal competence and performance
	Compensation related to real results

A recurring theme in many such diagnoses is that rigid bureaucracy is the culprit. The solution is to redesign the organizational structure, making it more flat and flexible. Reports usually end with a claim of a sense of urgency. It is time that the proposed changes are implemented, which will send a signal that change is seen as serious and unstoppable. Consistent with the programs described in Chapter I, champions are appointed. Elaborate communication schemes are implemented, and there is a flurry of activity and energy. After a year or two, the energy often dissipates and the organizations return to many of their defensive routines.

The trouble with this strategy is the same as that identified with the workshops on leadership in Part I and the diagnostic procedures just described, typical of performance appraisals. At best, the diagnoses describe valid causes of the problems, but do not get at how they are to be implemented. For example, the Model I theories-in-use, the skilled unawareness, the skilled incompetence, the generic counterproductive cycles, and the organizational defensive routines are bypassed. People may be aware of the bypass, and may also attribute that top management intends to cover up the bypass. They too cover up their doubts. As long as these actions occur, it is unfair to place the blame on hierarchy and bureaucracy. Individuals using Model I theories-in-use will create a behavioral world that is consistent with bureaucracy.

In one large organization, part of the kickoff process was a one-week workshop attended by its top forty executives. One of the presenters was a world-class lecturer on leadership. He conversed with the group for nearly six hours on the difference between managing and leading. His session was rated by the executives as one of the best.

I then met with the top twelve executives of this group for three three-hour sessions to discuss important business problems. Their dialogue was largely consistent with managing, not leading. Yet, the day before, these executives had evaluated the session as outstanding. They appeared unaware of the gap and inconsistency. The senior human resources vice president, however, recognized the gap and firmly "requested" the facilitators not to explore it. The reasoning was "timing." The gap would be discussed, he promised, at a subsequent session. Several such sessions were held during the next three years. The gap was, to my knowledge, never discussed. This did not surprise some of the senior executives reporting to the top group. One repeated the phrase, "The more things change, the more they stay the same."

I had the opportunity to observe another top management group. The leader was an executive who not only espoused Model II actions, he actually implemented them. He was highly respected by the new team members. "We don't have many like him." During a session, there was discussion about tough, productive reasoning that produces compelling arguments. One of the members asked me to illustrate my perspective by providing examples from the group discussion. I began with the way the CEO had crafted his argument on issue X. I concluded that the argument was not as compelling as I had heard him make in other settings. I illustrated my evaluation and asked for their reactions.

The CEO responded, first, by agreeing with me. There were gaps in his reasoning because of promises made to the board of directors, some of which he was not at liberty to state at this time. He encouraged me and others to continue their tough inquiry. If he could not answer, he would say so. He also added that he did not expect "designed censorship" to occur frequently because that would undermine his credibility.

During the break, one senior executive told me that he found my comments to be "a bit harsh" and unfair. After all, the CEO was under terrible pressure and what he needed was support. My recollection of the conversation that followed was something like:

Consultant: I appreciate your telling me of your evaluation. Is there anything that I said or did that prevented you from saying it in the group?

Senior Executive: (Smiling) I could say that a break was called, but that would not be correct. To be candid, I never even thought of saying it in front of the group. In this (organizational) culture, I am sure that would be considered inappropriate.

Consultant: Yes, I can sympathize with your concern. But how about the other side of the issue? If you had intervened, would not the CEO have felt supported? Perhaps other members felt as you did. Would he then not feel doubly supported?

Senior Executive: I suppose he would. But again, it never entered my mind to do so.

The senior executive in question was one of the highfliers and a vocal leader about changing the culture. He was always advocating that it was time that all learned to be more candid. Yet, when that time came to be more candid, he not only was silent but felt that he would be genuinely supported by the group for acting this way. He was skillfully unaware of the positive consequences if he had spoken and the negative consequences for not speaking. All this occurred when the person in error was acting as a consultant and the meeting was chaired by a CEO whom all the reports rated very highly.

After the break, he and I repeated the conversation to the group. It led to others admitting that they had similar views about my actions. Others disagreed. The CEO sided with the latter group. He requested that they not "support" him by remaining quiet. More important, he would hope that they would come to learn that he did not require such support. He added that if others could also come to feel this way, then group norms would be created for the kind of openness that was required around difficult issues.

This type of reflection and action, in my opinion, does more to change the culture than the "get-honest" pleas by top management or the outward-bound programs intended to create trust. Most of the members in this group had participated in these types of experiences and many evaluated them positively. These consequences, as we have just seen, were not transferred to this meeting where the "new" trust was needed.

The reason is that these types of change exercises do little to alter the Model I theories-in-use or the organizational defensive routines. Genuine organizational change and the new performance appraisal processes cannot occur under these conditions. The executives may feel better or closer, but this should not support the transformation that they espouse. Again, this claim can be tested by observing business sessions back home.

Conclusion

For genuine progress to occur in performance appraisals, we must realize that appraisals are going on all the time. The challenge is to enable these appraisals to surface as they are being made by any member of the group and thus also reveal a good deal of hidden information. For example, when we discussed the executive's evaluation of my evaluation of the CEO's reasoning, the group members learned that the CEO did not wish to be protected, that he was quite capable of listening to negative feedback, as long as it was crafted effectively, and that he wished that these and other features could become true for everyone and thereby change the group dynamics. Thus, self-reflection and appraisal becomes the basis for more effective problem solving as well as a group culture that facilitates learning, especially double-loop learning.

Many of the more difficult top-management performance problems are rarely individual problems. Group members have so much to learn from each other. But, even if there are individual performance problems, a group can facilitate helping that individual improve her or his performance. Elsewhere (Argyris 1993), I describe an experiment that a CEO and his immediate reports undertook to appraise the performance of the CEO.

I am proposing that human beings learn Model II theories-in-use, Model II social virtues, and Model II dialogues. This will lead to more effective dialogues not only about human issues but also about technical and business issues that are often suppressed by defensive routines of individuals, groups, intergroups, and organizational cultures.

I am also proposing that these changes become part of all long-range change programs in going through these various educational experiences. The individuals automatically become agents for change, not simply respondents of a shift that has already happened. Indeed, it should not be possible to make an informational double-loop cultural change without individuals learning new theories-in-use and new social virtues.

I believe that the signal virtue of the performance appraisal processes that I am recommending is that they can be produced in real time by monitoring observable behavior in the here and now. I also believe that under these conditions the players are best able to design the connection they wish to make between the performance review and the level of compensation.

9

Generating Internal Commitment to Values

VALUES FORM THE CORE of any organization. And while the values that each firm organizes around will differ, a great deal of agreement exists among popular business book authors and even some academics about how to create commitment to a set of values within an organization. Nearly all of them suggest something akin to the following:

- Define the values clearly.
- Communicate the values with the use of a multimedia network.
- Have senior executives, and other powerful people, champion the values.
- Make sure that employees understand the values and accept them.

Often authors advise that many meetings take place in which the employees participate in the definition of the values. And although the intention of these meetings clearly is to involve as many employees as possible, they are, by definition, only going to involve a relatively small number of them. So, besides being time consuming, these meetings are unlikely to produce a sustained internal commitment to the stated values for the organization as a whole.

Let us review the concept of internal commitment to understand why. Internal commitment is created when individuals have a significant influence on defining the goals to be achieved and the paths required to achieve them, when the goals represent a significant (but not insurmountable) challenge, and when all these are related to the central values and needs of the individuals.

It is possible to generate such a commitment among the individuals who are involved in defining the goals, values, aspirations, and actions necessary to achieve these goals. The problem is that the remaining employees who are of necessity left out of this commitment-building process will be externally committed to the values and goals. For these employees a significant gap will exist.

This suggests a second step. Make the gaps as explicit as possible and educate the individuals so that they can learn to fill those gaps. I will illustrate how this can be achieved by using an example of an organization in which a small group defined the values and, although the employees liked and even espoused those values, a significant gap continued to exist.

Closing the Gap in a Consulting Firm

The intervention took place in a large management consulting firm that has been, and continues to be, at the forefront of defining its values and striving to generate internal commitment to them (Argyris 1993). About 120 consultants who were employees for at least a year attended a workshop to increase their knowledge about the various services that the firm was selling to clients. A half-day was scheduled to deal with the challenge of making the values "come alive" in the firm.

The consultants completed a two-part questionnaire. In the first part, they were asked to evaluate the values, state their commitment to them, and express any doubts or concerns that they may have about implementing them. In their responses, all the consultants stated that they understood the values and expressed strong agreement with them. The communication schemes seemed to be working. However, the consultants expressed concerns about taking the values that they espoused and infusing them in their everyday existence. In short, they were having trouble making the values come alive. This concern was expressed even though the consultants agreed that the values were communicated clearly, that powerful senior members of the firm were acting as champions of these goals, and that the consultants understood and accepted the values.

In short, everything that the authors of business books suggest should happen, did happen. Yet significant concerns and gaps still existed. They can be categorized into three groups: concerns about others, about the firm, and about themselves. Let's look at each category individually.

Concerns about Others

- Could I jeopardize my reputation and career if I am forthright and candid with others?

- Could my superiors evaluate me negatively, but cover up that they are doing so?
- Is it possible to be so conscious of the values that they can be activated in every situation in which they are relevant?
- Will my superior back me up when I take responsibility for my choices?
- How do we produce honest communication when I experience a senior consultant saying different things around important topics such as allocation?

Concerns about the Firm

- How can any firm enforce values such as courage, openness, respect, and community?
- What is the impact of bonuses on internal competitiveness?
- Does speed on cases force sloppy analysis and conclusions?
- Would we work for tobacco companies who hide information and advertise to children?
- Could the firm's emphasis on choice and responsibility lead to conditions in which people feel undirected and lost?
- How can rewards be given on the basis of individual performance when responsibility is so diffuse?
- How can we innovate when the client is paying for results, not R&D?
- Won't client pressures and work demand compromise the values?
- Will the concept of "up or out" engender a politicized environment?

- Is the firm's emphasis on self-responsibility and individual choice likely to endanger its efforts to build a sense of community?

Concerns about Self

Significantly fewer respondents focused on the likely difficulties in making the values come alive because of some features of themselves or their fellow consultants. Those who did had the following concerns.

- Many of us espouse personal growth, yet we consistently evaluate how we stack up relative to others.
- If we reduce our own competitiveness, could we increase our effectiveness?
- If we just let go, will we compromise our values?
- I like the idea that reward is based on individual achievement and merit. I do not want anyone else rewarded for what I do, nor do I want to be rewarded for what others do.

Reflecting on the Concerns

The concerns expressed by the consultants are similar to those expressed by the directors. For example, the directors would not want the consultants to be evaluated negatively and the evaluations to be kept secret on the pretext that making them public will open up a can of worms and upset those involved. Similarly, the directors would want the consultants supported when they are acting consistently with the stated values of the firm, even if doing so would upset others.

The directors also agreed with the concerns that the consultants had about the firm's policies. For example, bonuses could produce competitiveness, envy, or feelings of unfairness. Pressure to get something done fast could produce sloppy work. Rewarding individual performance could be difficult when consultants work in teams and each person's contribution becomes entangled with the group's.

Finally, the directors agreed that many of the consultants were competitive and that this would likely create difficult interpersonal consequences within case teams. We have, therefore, a good deal of agreement about the barriers to making the values come alive.

A closer examination of these concerns reveals two important features. First, the concerns are likely to be activated at the local level and will therefore have to be managed at that level. Controls conceived at the top, if they were to capture the richness and complexity of the situation at the local level, would have to be so comprehensive and powerful that they would likely inhibit effective action. Firm policies and practices, like values and visions, can provide important frameworks, but the management of local actions is best accomplished by players at the local level.

The second concern is the built-in conflict between policies. For example, can the "up-or-out" policy intended to reward meritocracy also exacerbate fears and competitiveness? Can reward for individual performance undermine group effectiveness? Certainly such questions are legitimate and their resolution depends on the quality of the dialogue among the players who are experiencing them at the local level.

But they cannot do it alone. The resolution of these dilemmas also depends on how top management supports local-level dialogues. In this case, the top managers assert that they will be supportive and the majority of consultants believe this assertion. What will this require? Among other things, it necessitates that the players involved frame their concerns in ways that include their likely causal responsibility in creating them. Judging from the responses in the questionnaires and the case example, the consultants did not do so. They framed the problem as if top management was responsible for resolving the concerns. To use the language of Chapter 1, they acted as pawns. They did so even though they did not like such a dependent role and even though they admitted that top management genuinely did not want them to act like pawns.

If the consultants were more aware of their possible personal causal responsibility, they might have framed their concerns as follows:

- How can I and others create a relationship in which not only my views are respected, but the way by which I craft them is discussable?
- How can I and others help to make what is typically undiscussable discussable?
- Whenever I expect management to back me up, do I encourage their not doing so when I am wrong?
- If bonuses are based on individual performance, how can we create a community in which our sense of individuality blossoms from our being interdependent?
- How do we design relationships in which we are left alone but not to the point where we feel undirected and

lost? How do we assess the possibility that our feelings of being lost and undirected are self-protective?

- How can we frame our consulting practice so that the client realizes that the best conditions by which to get value added are to conduct R&D that is directly connected to results?
- If we agree that a meritocracy requires some form of "up or out," how do we implement it in such a way that is fair but, at the same time, does not protect the incompetent?
- If we are committed to the firm's values (because we believe that they are right) and if we realize most client firms—at best—espouse such values, how do make these values come alive in our firm and in the firms of clients who wish to make them come alive?
- How do we deal with the dilemma that, in order to evaluate and value our personal growth, we require information about how we stack up relative to others?
- Under what conditions does personal competitiveness inhibit *and* encourage consulting effectiveness?

The likelihood of an effective dialogue increases when the concerns are framed in this way because the consultants accept their responsibilities for not making the values come alive. Top management would not be faced with consultants whose framing of concerns placed the full responsibility in their lap. In my experience, such framing makes the top understandably wary about getting into a dialogue with the consultants.

In order to generate processes and practices that help the

values come alive, the top will first have to overcome the belief that consultants hold that this is almost exclusively the responsibility of the top management. This represents a challenge because the top management is likely to be faced with consultants who, because of their skilled incompetence and unawareness, could easily join together to reinforce and sanction the strategy of projecting the blame on others.

For example, in a situation I wrote of some years ago, a case team leader asked for a meeting to examine why the case team's performance was not as good as it had been in solving similar problems in the same company (Argyris 1990b). The sessions were tape-recorded. For three hours or so the consultants blamed the "stupid clients" and the fact that the case team leader was difficult to find.

I then asked if the consultants acted in ways that compromised their performance. Several immediately said that this was possible. However, none could come up with any examples. They were not even aware that their seeing the clients as stupid and anti-learning had important consequences. The latter sensed the unsurfaced negative views and many defended themselves by calling the clients young, naive, and full of themselves. Of course, they too covered up these evaluations.

The second feature is that these difficult challenges—challenges that exist in most organizations—are not likely to be resolved through the use of Model I theories-in-use. As we have seen, these tend to produce self-sealing, non-learning dialogues that leave all parties feeling misunderstood, frustrated, and helpless.

We can observe how these consequences did occur by returning to the second component of the questionnaire that the consultants completed. In it was a description of a case team leader (CTL) who dealt with a consultant in a manner that was hostile, unilaterally controlling, and suppressing of the consultant's views. In short, the CTL was clearly violating the values of the firm.

The consultants were asked to express their views of what was going on in the case. Not surprisingly, they all expressed negative evaluations of the CTL. Most of the reactions were highly to moderately negative. A few expressed a low intensity of anger. For example:

1. **Highly Negative**
    - I feel angry and demotivated.
    - CTL is a schmuck
    - CTL does not care about me or my work.
    - This pisses me off.
    - I feel helpless and powerless.
2. **Moderately Negative**
    - My work is belittled.
    - I feel discouraged.
    - CTL does not respect my abilities.
    - CTL is self-protective; hiding true thoughts.
3. **Low Negative**
    - This is unfair.
    - CTL may be under pressure.
    - Did I misunderstand?
    - Where could I have gone wrong?

The respondents with highly negative reactions combined their strong negative feelings with attributions that the CTL is wrong and closed to having an effective dialogue. Hence, they would feel helpless, powerless, and demotivated. For example, the CTL is in power, the CTL is arrogant, or the CTL is unjust in order to protect himself.

The CTL is written off, but the consultants say that they would cover up doing so. They act in ways that they condemned when describing their concern. For example, they expressed the fear that people in power would make negative judgments about them and cover up that they are doing so. They, too, made negative judgments about the CTL and would cover them up.

Moreover, in most cases, those who had strong and moderately negative feelings reported that, if they did not succeed in correcting the CTL, they would go to the appropriate superior and ask that they never be assigned to work with the CTL. They also said that they would cover up these actions from the CTL. These acts compound the inconsistency just identified.

There is another problem. How likely is it that the consultants are able to craft competent dialogue to correct the CTL if, as they report, they entered a situation thinking:

- Do I really believe enough in my work to risk shooting myself?
- What if I am wrong? But, hell, I'm not an idiot. Let's give it a try.
- I will make the CTL hear me before I change my position.
- I would obey if I had a genuine opportunity to explain my position.

Making Values "Come Alive"

A session was held in which the diagnosis made above was presented to the consultants. The first phase was to surface their reactions. In one such session, the consultants had little difficulty in validating the diagnosis about their concerns and the fact that top management had the same concerns.

The consultants had more difficulty in accepting responsibility for the dilemmas. For example, they claimed it would be unjust for the CTL to harm their career and take covert actions, yet the action strategies they put forward suggested they might do those very same things. The main thrust of the dialogue was to ask the consultants who doubted the validity of the diagnosis developed from the CTL case to role play how they would deal with the CTL. Several consultants tried. Their colleagues evaluated the dialogue as being akin to Model I. The next step was for the leaders of the session to role play alternatives that were akin to Model II. This provided the consultant with the opportunity to practice crafting different approaches. They found that they could do so, but they needed much more skill if Model II actions were to become part of their theory-in-use.

Learning opportunities were designed so that the consultants could learn Model II productive reasoning and skills. Other learning opportunities were designed in which they could practice their newly developed competencies with CTLs.

A different set of learning experiences could be developed around actual case team effectiveness. For example, case teams could meet with their respective CTLs periodically to examine their performance. In principle, these reflections could occur with case teams that included client members.

Reflecting on these strategies, we can see how it is possible to help make the values come alive. The foundation of the strategy is to develop a diagnosis that identifies both concerns *and* the degree to which consultants develop a perspective consistent with being a pawn. The consultants can then be helped to see that this perspective will not lead to making the values come alive.

Finally, as a result of becoming more effective in creating Model II dialogues, the consultants and their leaders will be able to create case teams that can take on more responsibility and control over their lives. These conditions are consistent with producing internal commitment at the local level.

Building Commitment Scenario 2:
The Case of Human Resources Professionals

A CEO, working with a small group, developed a document describing a vision of the organization and a set of values to help the vision come alive. The senior resources vice president (VPHR) sent the document to fifty human resource professionals throughout the company worldwide. He scheduled a meeting with them in order to evaluate the document and give helpful feedback to the CEO before the final document was communicated throughout the organization.

The overall reaction to the CEO's memo was a mixture of negative criticism and disbelief. They did not feel that the top really believed in the values in the document that the CEO and others created. The VPHR recommended that their doubts be communicated to the CEO and the group. The human resources professionals balked—it would be too dangerous. After a lengthy discussion, someone asked why they were worried. He thought that the CEO would not be surprised by their comments. Another added that if the fifty believed in these values, a meeting with the CEO could be a sign that they were trying to implement the values.

The CEO was invited. She accepted the invitation, but asked to see what values they would suggest. The human resources professionals took up the challenge. After they wrote their responses, they found that their ideas were also abstract and distanced from everyday life and that of the organization.

The meeting was held and it was highly rated by all who participated because people began by facing up to their defenses. The CEO admitted that she often acted in ways that dis-empowered the human resources professional. She did so because she was frustrated by them. They were quick to give her advice. Yet, when they were continuously challenged, they were unable to act consistently with their own advice. Shades of Tom and the CPs described in Part I.

One of the results was that a smaller group of twenty-four designed and implemented a workshop in which, by beginning with the left-hand–right-hand case method, they surfaced and engaged their Model I theories-in-use, their adherence to Model I social virtues, and their compliance with organizational defensive routines. This led to their realizing that they espoused Model II skills and consequences in the areas of leadership, change, and learning, yet their theory-in-use was largely Model I. They then turned to many months of effort to redesign many of the workshops. Included in the new workshops were opportunities for participants to examine the new values, the degree to which top management behaved consistently with them, and the degree to which they acted consistently with them. Becoming aware of their own gaps and inconsistencies led to a commitment to become more vigilant in everyday life to correct this. The basis for commitment was internal.

10

Generating Internal Commitment to Implementing Strategy

HOW CAN WE CREATE internal commitment to the development and implementation of competitive strategy? I should like to answer this question with two illustrations.

Illustration 1

Strategy is an important tool that executives use to make their world more manageable. It contains a core set of ideas about how to define the business and how to define success; about what the best techniques are for analyzing the external environment and external capabilities, generating alternative choices, identifying strategic options, developing scenarios, and testing options. Making such judgments requires productive reasoning. For example, premises are made explicit, data are collected rigorously, and inferences and conclusions are tested by logic that is not self-sealing.

However, in strategy making, there are two ways that people try to be in control, especially when the environment is threatening. They try to be in control of the technical ideas that require individuals to be rigorous and analytical and to test their ideas in ways that are not self-sealing. Or they try to be in control of the human dimension—making sure others are not heard, doing a hard sell to higher-ups on their particular strategy to blunt criticism and inquiry.

Complicating matters is the fact that when line or strategy professionals frustrate each other, both activate their respective theories of control, which is likely to intensify the defensiveness, increase the frustration, hasten the bypass, and deepen the cover-up.

Ironically, the ideas about how to be in control in the face of embarrassment and threat are themselves embarrassing. The implementation of the human theory of control violates the technical theory of control—that is, the best possible strategies are not put to the best possible tests—if participants are shut out and/or the process is rigged to garner acquiescence.

Whenever this occurs, it creates still more embarrassment and threat, which leads to further bypass and cover up. All these actions and reactions are highly skillful; hence the people involved are often unaware of their impact. If it happens that they are aware of the negative impact, they typically blame the organizational defensive routines. They report that they are in a double bind, unable to change their behavior.

To cope with this multidimensional problem, I joined with a professor of strategy to create a learning experience. We set out to teach "the best" in strategy development and implementation and to help participants see how they unknowingly shoot themselves (as well as their strategy) in the foot whenever they use the theories of control to deal with embarrassment and threat. Finally, the course was designed to help participants learn to correct and prevent such errors.

Educational activities were therefore designed to cover:

1. The core concepts of competitive strategy.
2. The conditions under which the implementation of strategy will be relatively straightforward.
3. The core concepts in the human theory of control.
4. The conditions under which the activation of these concepts will necessarily lead to the distortion, if not sabotage, of the strategic implementation.
5. The connection of these four domains of learning with every individual as well as with the actions of these individuals as a team. A key objective was to make the participants aware of their particular theory of human control, their team's theory, and their organizational defensive routines; and to teach them how these factors can hold strategy formulation and implementation hostage to designed error.

One Learning Environment

The following is a brief description of the learning environment we created for four top-management groups. Each group had the authority to design and (with approval of the top board) implement a strategy.

The First Step: Collecting Data

Our teaching method began with visits to the top-management teams at their respective locations. The teams outlined their thoughts about the strategic problems they wished to solve. They worked out what background information they should prepare to bring to the conference center. Several weeks before the session, the teams sent a document to the two faculty members outlining the work they had done and what they intended to accomplish during the five-day session at the conference center. Each member was also asked to write a brief case about an important human problem that he or she expected to face in implementing the strategy. The cases were mailed to me about three weeks before the sessions were to begin.

Professor Saias, the strategy expert I worked with on this case, and I met for one day before the session to identify the key strategic and human problems that would arise. This exercise influenced what ideas each of us would present at the outset as well as the areas in which we each could connect with the other's discipline when describing his own views.

The Second Step: Control

During the first day of the conference, we focused on providing the key concepts of our respective disciplines as they related to the problems that were illustrated by the cases. The first three-hour session was on strategy. I attended the session with the specific aim of noting any challenges the participants might raise regarding whether the strategic concepts being taught could be implemented. For example, a participant could say, "These ideas make sense, but we cannot use them in our organization." Professor Saias, whose discipline was strategy, would ask the participant what might prevent their use. As the behavioral faculty member, I would follow up with questions about the individual and organizational defenses implied in the question or answer.

The second three-hour session was on organizational defensive routines: how they can limit learning, and how limited learning can lead to strategy discussions with gaps and inconsistencies that go unrecognized or undiscussed. This sparked a spirited discussion often punctuated with examples from the participants' organizations. Toward the end of the session one of the general managers remarked on how productive it would be if "all of us could commit to reducing these defenses." Personally," he said, "I believe they are my nemesis around strategy—indeed, around most of the difficult issues that we discuss."

The Third Step: Formulating and Implementing Strategy

Each team went into a small room to begin formulating, designing, and planning for implementation of their respective strategies. When defensive routines (organizational or individual) arose, they were treated as a matter of legitimate inquiry.

The groups began to examine the impact of organizational and individual defensive routines sooner than we had expected. For example, Group A's general manager started by reviewing the strategic thrust that had been developed so far, the questions yet to be answered, and the implementation issues to be discussed. After he finished his introduction he asked for comments. One executive asked, "Are we to take the ideas on organizational defensive routines seriously?"

The general manager answered, "Of course. If you recall, I was the one who ended the plenary session by saying they were important. Indeed, I think I called them my nemesis."

"Yes, I was pleased to hear you say that, and I wanted to check to make sure you still felt that."

"I most certainly do."

The executive then said that in the spirit of making "undiscussable topics discussable," he wanted to question the direction of the strategy developed so far. As he continued to speak, it became clear that he was asking for a major change.

The general manager became very upset and asked, "What the devil is going on? I thought the major directions of our strategy had been agreed upon."

The facilitator intervened to ask the executive what he was feeling and thinking as he heard the general manager's reaction. The executive said that the response confirmed his fears: the general manager wanted individuals to be candid—up to a point. "I think that I may have made an error in raising the question," the executive said.

The general manager apologized, saying he realized that he was violating what he espoused in the plenary session and in his first response to the executive's question. "But you know," he said, "it is not easy to hear this."

"Yes," responded the executive, "and it is not easy to say it."

The general manager then encouraged others to speak. Several agreed with the executive. The facilitator asked, "What normally goes on at these meetings that leads people to hold back on such data?" The responses were candid. Participants described several organizational defensive routines involving "going along" with a higher-level executive when they believed that the supervisor was wrong but was also emotionally committed to his or her position. For example, one said, "I saw you [the general manager] as wanting this strategy. This is your baby. The strategy makes good sense and thus is not easy to refute. I figured given your strong commitment to it and the lack of support that I would get from others, it made sense to go along. I must say, I did not realize until now that others had similar doubts."

When we examine this incident, we see a group describing defensive routines that "caused" several members to withhold technical ideas about strategy. Group members also described defensive routines that prevented them from testing their understanding of what issues could be discussed.

The general manager's initial reaction of dismay and bewilderment was an example of an individual defensive routine. His reaction was inconsistent with what he had been espousing, and was automatic and skillful. As the discussion continued, some group members also became aware of their individual protective reactions, which were to withdraw and distance themselves from situations that could be embarrassing or threatening. Other examples of defensive routines, though perhaps not as dramatic, could have been presented. All groups made significant alterations to the technical thrust of their strategy after certain relevant defensive routines were revealed. This occurred most often when issues of implementation were discussed. It appeared that when some players disagreed with substantive features of strategy but felt that these could not be easily challenged, they waited until the moment came to discuss their implementation. They could then raise questions about the viability of the technical ideas. Often this led to an examination of organizational defensive routines that had not surfaced earlier.

For example, one general manager opposed a strategic thrust, not taking into account that he believed it was not likely to be implemented. When he consciously considered the probable organizational resistance to it, he was compelled to rethink his position. With the help of the facilitator, the group also examined why some participants did not think about the resistance that might occur and why some felt they could challenge technical ideas only by waiting until their implementation was discussed. Often this meant technical issues that were not discussed would be challenged hours later.

The Fourth Step: Implementation

The groups also discussed the cases written by the participants. In summary, the participants became aware of their personal human theory of control. They saw how it made them poor learners under conditions in which learning was important. They also became aware of how unaware they had been of the discrepancy between what they meant to accomplish and what they actually produced.

This learning occurred at several levels. The first level involved becoming aware of the inconsistencies and gaps that one produced through one's behavior. For example, participants believed that it is important to be candid, forthright, and straightforward. But they were candid and forthright in a way that discouraged others from being the same, and they were unaware of this consequence while producing it. Further, the participants believed that it is a good idea to identify an error in order to correct it. They were often unaware that they were producing interpersonal errors *and* that they were communicating to others that they were unaware. In addition, they believed that it is a good idea to test the validity of ideas, especially if they are controversial. Yet the tests they themselves used were weak and often self-serving.

Each participant also learned why the others did not discuss his or her inconsistencies and gaps: Because the participant was perceived as being unaware, to discuss them could be embarrassing for him or her. The others covered up the participant's inconsistencies and acted as if they were not doing so. Sometimes their cover-ups succeeded; other times they did not. In almost all cases in which they did not, the target of the cover-up also covered up the fact that he or she felt like a target.

The second level of learning involved realizing the dilemmas and paradoxes that resulted from one's behavior. For example, the participants who acted unilaterally (whether they realized it or not) did so because it was consistent with their personal theory of human control; however, for that feature of their theory of control to work, the *recipient* of their behavior had to act in a submissive manner—which is the kind of behavior the first participants considered ineffective.

The third level involved learning that the actions at the first two levels combined to create group and organizational defensive routines that led to self-reinforcing patterns.

The next level involved learning that the first three levels combined to cause individuals to massage, distort, and/or censor technical information related to strategy. Their doing so produced conditions in which important technical and business information tended to be inaccessible, ambiguous, and/or vague. Productive reasoning was dominated by defensive reasoning.

Identifying these consequences was itself liberating for the participants because most of them had believed that they were "undiscussable." Examining this issue led individuals to make public their private views about what constituted acceptable behavior in the group and the organization whenever the potential for embarrassment or threat existed. This discussion made it possible for the participants to interrupt the cycles that they had felt could not be interrupted. Moreover, it enabled them to identify ways to avoid these self-sealing ruts.

Finally, individuals began to learn (1) how to craft their conversations so they could act consistently with the new norms, and (2) how to see when they were not acting consistently. All this learning was continually tested against the task of solving real business problems. Whenever someone asked, "Is all this really necessary?" the answer was another question: "If we do not change, how will we transfer business information that is now inaccessible and ambiguous into information that is accessible and clear?"

By the way, once these new norms were created—once ongoing learning was legitimized—the learning was transferable, within these groups, to any business subject.

The Fifth Step: Continued Learning

As the week progressed, the boundary separating the technical and the behavioral began to blur. For example, in several groups, members significantly changed their substantive positions on strategy. They had had enough successful experiences in their "behavioral" sessions, which dealt with organizational defensive routines, that they could begin to confront problems in their strategy group that they previously had covered up.

As the participants talked about running silent and running deep, important technical information surfaced that changed their outlook on strategy formulation. By the third day, the integration between the behavioral and the strategic had gone beyond our expectations. Professor Saias and I found ourselves being scheduled for discussions and meetings during lunch, through dinner, and into the late hours of the evening.

The Sixth Step: Implementation

The groups returned to their respective organizations and began to implement features of their strategies.

The Seventh Step: Follow-Up

Six months later, the groups returned for a three-day session. Several groups had new members. Professor Saias and I had designed a crash "catch-up" course for the new members, but it failed because the course did not provide the in-depth learning that had been available to their colleagues. Next time, we will allocate more time to teaching new participants. It is fair to add, however, that the new members were able to learn some things faster because they were in a group that had developed skills for on-line learning and established norms to permit reflection on action.

During these sessions the groups continued to modify their strategic plans and, especially, to monitor the plans' implementation. In one group, several senior executives focused on how frustrated and concerned they were about the impact of the implementation. They believed that the sales structure they had created might well be counterproductive. They also discussed how unaware they had been of some of its consequences. It had taken them six months of implementation to identify problems that they had not foreseen.

I should like to highlight two features of this discussion. First, the group discussed matters that would have been undiscussable six months earlier. The sales executives, for example, would have been hesitant to discuss openly how blind they had been about the problems of implementation. They also would have been unwilling to admit that the frustrations of implementation were leading them to change their minds about the technical strategic thrusts to which they had agreed.

The second feature is the discussion of "deeper" problems. For example, the CEO and several others had been hesitant to take the sales executive's concerns about strategy seriously because they perceived that he felt frightened about the changes. They did not wish to base changes in strategy on reasoning used by an executive they believed was frightened. Moreover, the CEO and several others explained that they were especially apprehensive about discussing such issues because they believed the sales executive was unaware of how frightened he sounded.

The sales executive was indeed surprised to hear this. He insisted, however, that he was not frightened. He said he was apprehensive, but not about himself so much as about the impact the new strategy was having on the organization. Having learned from the session, he asked his fellow team members what he had said or done that had led them to believe he was personally apprehensive. They were able to provide him with concrete examples that helped him to think about how to craft his conversation to express more accurately his apprehension about the organization.

Notes on Effectiveness

The systematic study of the program's effectiveness will have to wait for the results of the research; however, several obser-

vations may be made at this time based on how the participants "voted" through their actions.

1. In all cases except one, the strategies were implemented
   and monitored in ways that participants described as
   effective. It is difficult to make an assessment of the
   fourth case because the company was sold and the participants did not return to the conference center.
2. The leaders of the three teams communicated to their
   managers that the learning experiences were helpful.
   They recommended further investments of time and
   money, even though both were significant. Moreover,
   they recommended that their managers (and their
   group) attend future sessions. Two of these managers
   have made plans to do so.
3. The participants saw the learning process as ongoing.
   For them, the boundaries separating education, team
   development, organizational development, and strategy
   have become fuzzy and irrelevant. The educational
   experience, in their eyes, respects the wholeness of
   their endeavor. It is the first time in the history of their
   corporations that senior line managers have pressed
   educational professionals to expand a program. It is also
   the first time that they are applying pressure at the corporate level to educate members of the corporation so
   they can emulate the skills of their two teachers.

Illustration 2

In the previous section, I illustrated how the making of strategic choices can be integrated with effective dialogue through

the use of the theory of action described in this book. The integration was carried out by experts in each area. The results, according to the top management groups who participated, were very helpful.

This team process can be effective when the two experts are able to create Model II relationships among themselves. What is likely to be more effective, however, is for the integration to occur within an individual. This is especially true when we wish to educate line management in these skills; they, after all, are responsible for the outcomes that are created.

The section by Roger Martin illustrates how this can be done.* The fundamental role of the theory of action concepts and skills is to reduce the barriers to structuring effective strategic choices. Martin presents a framework for structuring choices in which Model II theory-in-use, Model II social virtues, and productive reasoning help to implement the strategic-choice processes more effectively.

What is also true, but less emphasized in his paper, is that his thinking about effective strategic choices was influenced by his awareness and skills in Model II and in productive reasoning. In other words, the development of the "technical" theory of strategic choice was influenced strongly by the "behavioral" theory of action.

In this paper, Martin illustrates how a theory of action perspective can be used to reduce the barriers to effective structuring of strategic choice. Martin illustrates how individual defensive reasoning, Model I theory-in-use, and Model I social virtues combined to create defensive routines during the dia-

---

*This case was developed by Martin while working with clients of the Monitor Company.

logue that help to assure flawed dialogue and flawed strategic choices. Flawed choice processes are produced when choices do not get framed properly, when real choices are not made, or when they are made but fall apart, and when the action is not timely. Barriers such as these can be reduced by using Model II theory-in-use, social virtues, and productive reasoning.

As Martin suggests, too often advice about producing sound choices is undermined, especially when the choices may be threatening to various players and there are conflicting views of what are appropriate and inappropriate choices. Martin provides several illustrations. The dueling logic is consistent with Model I rules, such as make your own inferences and do not test them. Or, if you test the inference, do so by using self-referential logic. If others call you on the use of self-referential logic, deny it and use fancy footwork that places the blame on others.

There are two strategies that can be used to reduce these counterproductive consequences. The first is, in effect, reduce the likelihood that Model I defensive reasoning and actions will be activated. The concept of reverse engineering is an example of a strategy that, if used correctly, can lead to a reduction of the defensive routines that jeopardize effective inquiry and dialogue.

Reverse engineering begins with asking the participants the question: How do they believe their competitors would react to the choices they made? In order to answer these questions, the participants will have to reflect and surface their views of the competitors and of themselves. Once an answer is developed that is acceptable to all, the participants then take on the next question, and so on. Such a scenario, if followed correctly, will help participants to reduce the counter-productive consequences described above.

But accepting the validity of the dueling concepts and using reverse engineering is not a guarantee that defensive reasoning and actions will not occur. It is important therefore to ask what is behind the defensive actions? Martin provides several answers. For example, in the case of the dueling relationship, each participant sees self as the conveyor of truth; his colleague as misinformed. The task is to get the colleague to see things "my way." Martin describes that with this framing, the participants assert their views without making their reasoning explicit, they discourage inquiry into their own views, blame others for the problems, and promote various fancy footwork defenses. Although the correct implementation of reverse engineering is designed to reduce these consequences, they may still occur if the use of Model I is strong and the organizational defensive routines are powerful. All these consequences are consistent with Model I theories-in-use, Model I virtues, and organizational defensive routines. It is these factors that drive the actions Martin describes as counterproductive.

These actions can be connected by framing the context and acting consistently with Model II. For example, the individuals believe they have a valuable point of view but they do not believe they understood everything. They believe that their colleagues may have access to data that is important. Corrective actions include advocating their views and encouraging inquiry into them, exploring mutual responsibility for errors, and promoting learning by providing constructive feedback.

In practice, these actions can be produced if the participants are skillful at Model II and the organizational defensive routines are minimal or are discussable and influenceable. Martin makes it clear that in order to produce the constructive dialogue that is required, individuals will have to learn to use Model II or its equivalent.

Finally, Martin is also clear that the organizational defensive routines will have to be reduced for dueling to be reduced and reverse engineering to be successful. I have observed Martin advise strategy professionals and line managers to take the five-step process by beginning with the step of framing the choice. Often many strategy professionals agree, but add that this strategy is not acceptable in the organization. They argue that they are forced, by line management or by approval-seeking senior strategy professionals, to take such counterproductive routines as studying issues.

Martin acknowledges that this is likely to happen. He then engages the audience in crafting what they would say to line management given a genuine opportunity to identify the likely counterproductive consequences of bypassing Step One. The responses crafted by the participants are consistent with Model I crafting or the opposite—that is, easing in. Martin helps them to recraft their strategies and try them out. He also states that the best solution is that top management use the five-step process themselves.

As I listen to the dialogue with the audience, most of them express genuine fears of "being honest." They provide examples in which the organizational defensive routines make it foolish to be honest. Martin again acknowledges this possibility and again helps them to see that the way they craft their "open" and "honest" statements leads to others' feeling closed but publicly hiding their defensive feelings. This is, in effect, consistent with Model I defensive dishonesty. We are back to the paradoxes described in Part I. Attempts at being open and honest, when crafted consistently with Model I, will lead to closedness and dishonesty, both of which are covered up.

It is important to emphasize that individuals produce these counterproductive actions even after they admit their actions are counterproductive and even after they want to reduce the counterproductive consequences. And, most important, when given a chance to craft their conversation in line with their new intentions, they fail and are unaware that they are failing. When they do become aware, they immediately blame the organizational defensive routines. The point is that even with a theory of making choices that the participants accept, even with the best intentions their actions are often consistent with defensive reasons and Model I.

We now can see how integrating strategy, through the use of strategic-choice structuring, with theories about effective leadership, learning, and internal commitment can be implemented by human beings who not only espouse these frameworks, but are also skillful at implementing them.

Take it one step further. It is possible to substitute strategic-choice structuring with other functional managerial disciplines, such as activity-based costing, marketing management, the use of information technology, and the introduction and implementation of new products. It is also possible to use a theory of action to produce the high-quality dialogue each of these activities requires if they are to be implemented effectively.

It follows that a generic educational process for effective leadership is to integrate the "technical" and "human" perspectives in a manner similar to the one Martin used. I believe that this is the next challenge for leadership, learning, and organizational change.*

• • •

At the root of all strategy lies the ability to make good choices. A company's strategy is defined by the multiple and varied choices it makes—choices about when and where to compete and how to win in the businesses it has chosen. For the most part the primary strategic choices that a company makes are exclusive. That is, a decision to go in one direction precludes setting off in another. A decision to stay focused on the North American market, for example, precludes becoming a truly global firm, while a decision to continue to sell through an existing distribution channel precludes a new initiative that takes the product directly to the consumer.

As these examples show, true choices require giving up one thing in order to reap the strategic benefits of the other. If multiple options can be pursued simultaneously or there is but one sensible option, the firm does not face a true strategic choice.

Choices, then, by definition are hard. And often the firm does not anticipate the need to make the choices it faces. Instead they appear unexpectedly like forks on a country road. They are driven by customers, competitors, technological change, regulatory change and sometimes even the prior actions of the company itself.

These developments produce options; they give rise to new demands from customers and new ways to approach and serve the market, and they necessitate immediate decisions. How-

———

*Martin is the author of pages 191–215.

ever, the firm does not always recognize that it has come upon a fork in the road, nor is it always cognizant of the reality that it will choose one of the branches, even if it does so by default.

What is a Good Choice?

It follows then that a good strategic choice is one made consciously and one based on valid data and sound reasoning. Most often it results from a process that builds the necessary commitment for action.

Good choices identify, and mobilize the company toward, the combination of market positioning and unique activities that represent the best scenario for where to play and how to win in a chosen market. In short, a set of good choices positions a firm for competitive advantage.

A bad choice, on the other hand, results in travel down a path that is not conducive to value maximization, a path that constrains future choices rather than opening up new possibilities. When a firm makes a sub-optimal choice, typically one consequence is that it can never work its way back to the position it was in before it made the wrong choice.

At Monitor, we have spent the past decade helping companies make good strategic choices. While it would be easy to assume that bad choices reflect bad judgment or a poor strategic outlook, in our experience, bad strategic choices result most often from flawed choice processes. Processes that don't properly identify choices, processes that don't lead to consensus in a timely manner or create real commitment. These flaws can be eliminated by paying careful attention and applying rigorous design to the choice-structuring process.

In this white paper, we will discuss the attributes of a high-quality strategic choice; the typical flaws in strategic choice processes that prevent high-quality strategic choices from being made; and an approach to strategic choice structuring that helps overcome those flaws.

ATTRIBUTES OF A HIGH-QUALITY STRATEGIC CHOICE

A high-quality strategic choice possesses four key attributes:

- It is genuine;
- It is sound;
- It is actionable; and
- It is compelling.

Genuine

In order for a choice to be genuine, it must be made between at least two viable options, and it must specify clearly what the firm will and will not do as a consequence. The company must choose where to play (which customers to serve, what needs to target) and where not to play, how to compete (how the firm will achieve advantage over competitors in the chosen customer groups or segments of the market) and how not to compete.

A choice that is not genuine does not clearly delineate what the company will and won't do as a result. For example, at one company with which we are familiar a six-month strategic review resulted in a committed decision to focus on the customer. Fair enough, but could the company really have decided otherwise? Could it ever truly choose to ignore the customer?

Probably not. In fact, the true test of a choice comes when a competitor decides to travel down the path not taken and succeeds with this alternative choice. Only then does a company truly have confirmation that a choice was faced and made.

Sound

A sound choice flows logically from the accumulated facts, figures and beliefs of the choice makers. Sound choices neither ignore nor rest on intuition. They are the product of good logic applied to accurate data—data which is representative and robust. In a well-thought-out choice making process, the logic applied to the data can be clearly articulated and easily tested.

Sound decisions are not overly influenced by the relationships or relative power positions of the key players, and as a result, they have a rigor that comes from sustained and open testing. Let me explain.

Any team of managers starts with various types of information—results, past experience, etc. Members of the management team select key facts from the pool of available data and then apply logic to that data in order to draw the inferences necessary to make a choice.

In order for the choice to be sound, the data upon which the decision is to be made must be valid. That is, the data used in the decision making must be representative of the universe from which they were drawn. Too often in these processes the data is mined to extremes in order to support a preordained conclusion.

In addition, these processes either do not allow any non-

MAKING STRATEGIC CHOICES

Data

Logic

Choice

quantitative data to be represented or they allow so many hunches to drive the process that things go askew. While many strategic decisions must be made on the basis of qualitative or 'soft' data—the salesman's experience of the customers, an engineer's understanding of a product's design features—this data, too, must be tested in a logical way, not just asserted.

Opinions, hunches and strong intuitions, after all, are simply conclusions drawn from experiences in the field, 20 years of watching a cyclical industry play out in good times or in bad, or the golden gut of a marketer. Far from being discarded, these intuitions—like the hard data in the spread sheets—need to be tested.

Typically there are many layers of inference among the data, the experience, and the recommended action or choice. This phenomenon can be illustrated on the 'ladder of inference' below.

This chain of logic must be made explicit and subjected to testing by the other members of the management team who may have alternative points of view. By vetting the logic in an open and challenging discussion, the logic chain is validated and a robust choice results.

Actionable

A choice is of little value unless it can be implemented. That means the choice can be easily communicated, can be broken down into a series of steps to be taken immediately, and can be further broken down into long-term achievable goals and doable tasks. It is possible, after all, to reduce inventory by 10 percent. It is less doable to ensure high quality without some clear sense of what it means.

LADDER OF INFERENCE

Decide what to do:
Innovation and leadership are the most critical avenues to pursue.

Understand / evaluate what is happening:
Customers will stick with us if we continue to innovate and lead.

Name the data:
Customers value leadership and innovation.

Paraphrase the data:
This customer values our leadership and innovation.

Select the data:
I really like VisionTech. It has been an innovative leader for a long time.

VisionTech Customer: I really like VisionTech. It has been an innovative leader in business for a long time. But I'm coming under increasing cost pressure and have to make tradeoffs.

Thanks to Chris Argyris for the "Ladder of Inference" framework.

Compelling

The choice must be sufficiently compelling to generate management commitment to the choice—not just in an abstract it makes sense kind of way, but in an engaged and energetic way. The commitment of the management team will be tested twice. First by subordinates, who will judge the enthusiasm of the management team by the way in which it communicates the choice, and who will also test the logic of the decision against their own experience of the market.

Second, as the choice is implemented, both managers and employees will watch as other competing firms take strategic paths they have rejected and be successful with those alternative choices (confirming that a genuine choice indeed has been made). At this point it will be tempting for a partially committed management team to deviate from its choice and chase after other business strategies (e.g., "the market leader just entered the market with product X; we must offer product X as well").

Hence the tests of a compelling choice are: Can the management team achieve sufficient commitment to make a choice to change direction? Can the team maintain sufficient enthusiasm to enable its employees to implement the choices? And can the managers put the strategy into action for long enough to achieve success?

OBSTACLES TO HIGH-QUALITY STRATEGIC CHOICE

Many factors can get in the way of good strategic choices: politics, bad analysis, turbulent markets. But in most cases flawed choices are the product of flawed processes.

> **In a flawed choice-structuring process:**
> - **Choices do not get framed.**
> - **Choices do not get made.**
> - **Choices appear to get made, but fall apart.**
> - **Choices are not sound.**
> - **Choices get made, but action is not timely.**

Choices Do Not Get Framed

Strategic choices rarely appear on the radar screen initially as choices. Instead they appear as issues, problems, challenges. For example, losing share in one's home market to a foreign competitor tends to appear on management's radar screen as a problem. The typical response to a problem, issue or challenge is to study and analyze it. However, when an issue is studied or analyzed as an issue, management might confirm (or not) the seriousness of the situation, achieve a more in-depth understanding of the issue, and bring a more clear definition to the issue, but not produce choice.

The difficulty is magnified when the management team hands the issue to a task force (whether an internal group or external consultants) to study. The task force tends to go off and study the problem as defined. It tends to form some sort of opinion based on the data it sees as salient and the inferences it sees as relevant. It reports back to the management team, typically just with data and analysis, but sometimes with a recommendation on actions to address the problem.

In the case where the report is just data and analysis, the management team is only marginally closer to a strategic choice. The choice has not yet been framed and the data and analysis produced by the task force may or may not be relevant to the choice that eventually must be contemplated to make the issue, challenge, problem go away. In the case of a recommendation, the task force frames the choice—either implicitly or explicitly—and produces a recommended option, but the management team is likely to see either the choice as inappropriately framed or the data and logic as less than compelling—despite the fact that the data is entirely compelling to the task force.

Thus, if the choice is not framed at the outset as a choice, the ensuing process is highly unlikely to produce concerted action despite the time-consuming and expensive efforts of the management team and the task force.

Choices Do Not Get Made

In cases where the management team does correctly frame the issue as a strategic choice, it may still fail to generate a choice because of fundamental disagreements among members of the management team.

Fundamental disagreements occur when each member of the management team applies his own pattern of inferences to his own accumulated data to reach a conclusion. Often team members can't articulate their logic or talk about the data that was most powerful to them in reaching their conclusion. As a result, individual members of the management team can reach conclusions that are highly contradictory. They develop 'dueling ladders of inference' even if they start out appearing to observe the same data, as in the example at right.

In this example, the two managers reach conclusions that are irreconcilable at that elevated level of inference. Neither

DUELING LOGIC

Sally decides what to do
Innovation and leadership are the most critical avenues to pursue.

Sally understands/evaluates what is happening
Customers will stick with us if we continue to innovate and lead.

Sally names the data
Customers value leadership and innovation.

Sally paraphrases the data
This customer values our leadership and innovation.

Sally selects the data
I really like VisionTech. It has been an innovative leader for a long time.

Bill decides what to do
We've got to keep our costs down so we can be price competitive.

Bill understands/evaluates what is happening
Customers will migrate away from us due to cost concerns and our pricing.

Bill names the data
Customers are feeling intense cost pressure.

Bill paraphrases the data
This customer is going to make a tradeoff against us because of cost pressure.

Bill selects the data
But I'm coming under increasing pressure and have to make tradeoffs.

VisionTech Customer: I really like VisionTech. It has been an innovative leader in business for a long time. But I'm coming under increasing cost pressure and have to make tradeoffs.

Thanks to Diana Smith of Action Design for the "Dueling Logic" framework.

manager can understand how the other got to his or her conclusion. Each begins to attribute that the other "simply doesn't get it." The participants either shout at each other from the tops of their ladders (i.e., at the conclusion level) or withdraw from the process, or shout first and then withdraw.

In either case, the management team tends to experience gridlock, which eventually causes them to abandon the choice (or miss the relevant window of choice) and allow the status quo to prevail. Reconciling the dueling ladders feels impossible, especially when the duel is not between just two managers but the many members of the management team, and the momentum of the current state simply wins out and no change is made.

This has negative consequences in both the short and long term. The short-term consequence is a bad immediate strategic choice. In the long term, if the management team continually runs into gridlock around strategic choices, the team can become fractionalized, and members will begin to distance themselves and withdraw from future decision-making processes.

Choices Appear To Get Made, But Fall Apart

In this scenario, the management team appears to reach consensus, but it is a false or weak consensus lacking the commitment necessary to drive action.

False consensus occurs when one or more members of the management team do not agree with the choice that emerges but do not reveal their concerns or discomfort to the group during the process. Often this is a mechanism for individuals to distance themselves in order to "get the process over with." Alternatively, it can result from a feeling of intimidation, a fear of reproach for making unpopular opinions public. If the concerns of these silent members are not voiced, the concerns cannot be resolved in the process and commitment cannot be built throughout the management team. The result: the silent but doubting members of the team drag their feet in implementation or work actively to subvert implementation.

Weak consensus occurs when one or more members of the management team have discomfort with the choice but believe that they have enough commitment to support implementation even if they have some doubts. Weak consensus of this sort tends to break down the moment the company hits the first bump in the road toward implementation. At this point, team members with weak commitment question the intelligence and validity of the choice and typically call for rethinking the choice based on the 'new data' that has come forward. The desire to rethink the choice tends to prevail and the earlier choice is negated.

Choices Are Not Sound

The fourth obstacle to good strategic choice is a process that does not produce sound choices. This can occur for one of two reasons: invalid data or substandard logic.

Invalid data is a problem when the process is rushed and the group members are forced to use only the data in hand—some of which is likely to be outdated. Similarly, if only a subset of the relevant managers is involved in the choice process, data that is salient to them but not to other relevant managers may dominate the considerations.

Substandard logic is a problem when there is no public testing of inferences. Testing of inferences is best done by a group of managers whose familiarity with the data and the business situation enables them to consider carefully the validity of each inference. For example, given the data from the customer interviews, what can we infer about the priorities for product development?

This testing is best performed when the management team works as a group and openly debates each team member's logic. If management team members fail to reveal their own logic or demur in challenging the logic of others, there is a high likelihood of producing substandard logic. Incomplete discussions of logic are often the result of subordinates fearing the consequences of questioning the logic of a more senior member of the management team.

Choices Get Made, but Action Is Not Timely

The final manifestation of a flawed choice-structuring process results when a choice is made, but not acted on in a timely way. This can happen for two primary reasons: First, the choice process can take so long that the choice is no longer timely. This is a variant of the inability-to-choose problem discussed above.

Second, the choice can be made by a subset of the relevant management team but then the selling process required for getting "buy-in" can take such an inordinate amount of time that the choice becomes obsolete (competitors have beat you to it, the problem has changed, etc.). In this case the flaw is in the selection of the group that works together to produce the choice. If the group does not include the breadth of managers necessary to drive action, then the process is almost guaranteed to produce a delay between choice and action as other constituents are brought on board.

A PROCESS FOR STRUCTURING STRATEGIC CHOICES

The goal of a choice-structuring process is to produce sound strategic choices that lead to successful action. The strategic choice-structuring process has five steps as follows:

- **Frame the choice.**
- **Brainstorm possible options.**
- **Specify conditions necessary to validate each option.**
- **Prioritize the conditions which create the greatest barrier to choice.**
- **Design valid tests for the key barrier conditions.**

Frame the Choice Clearly

Amalgamated Paper (AP) has been experiencing low profitability at its kraft pulp mill on the West Coast for some time. The mill drifts in and out of cash-operating loss depending on the pulp price cycle. Closing the mill is not an easy option for two reasons: First, the mill is an integral part of the West Coast operations. If it were closed, the government would be almost certain to retaliate against AP by taking away its timber cutting rights which would be devastating for the rest of the West Coast operations. Second, the West Coast has always been considered an integral part of AP's core business. Any reduction in the scale and scope of the West Coast operation would lead Wall Street analysts to doubt AP's overall strategy. More importantly, the mill has long been an important asset to AP—closing it would be a blow to corporate morale and a huge drain on the economy around it. So the problem remained as a problem—how to deal with the profitability problem on the West Coast—even after three studies.

The first step in choice structuring is to frame the issue as a choice. This involves looking beyond the problem to discern the type of tradeoff the problem embodies and hence the type of choice required in order to solve it. Until a minimum of two mutually exclusive options are identified that would neutralize the issue/problem, the choice is not framed. Until a choice is framed, it cannot be made.

Three key members of the management team (CEO, VP Strategy, VP R&D) were convened to consider the West Coast problem. They concluded that the status quo would surely produce continued low and variable profitability which would depress the earnings of the overall firm. They came to the conclusion that AP either had to invest more in the West Coast, divest, or significantly restructure its West Coast operations through merger/joint venture to make the problem go away. At this point, they had framed the problem as a choice, and the challenge now was to make that choice.

It was critical at that early stage, and at each successive stage, to involve the individuals who will be taking action in order to build commitment. The three-person team recognized that it needed to broaden immediately to five managers by adding the head of the pulp business unit whose mill was central to the deliberations and the head of the paper business, who would be involved in any possible forward integration into paper products at the site of the mill.

Brainstorm Options

The second step in the choice-structuring process is to create an inclusive list of viable options. The initial step of framing the issue as a choice identified a subset of options, but now, with an appropriate group of managers, the task is to broaden the list.

The objective in this step is to be inclusive rather than restrictive of the number and diversity of options on the table. Later in the process the team will hone and prune the list. At this stage, it is important not to trivialize or dismiss options—everything is fair game. The later steps of the choice-structuring process will weed out options that are not viable.

An option should be thought of as a story, a story that describes how the firm could choose a place in the market to play and a way to win against competition. These stories derive from the individual interpretations of managers as to how the market functions (what customers will want, what competitors will do, how the future of the industry will likely evolve, etc.). At this point in the process, the standard of rigor applied to the stories is mild. If the story has internal logical consistency and results in the firm's winning in the market, it should be included as an option. If, however, it is not possible to tell a story of why a given action (e.g., focus on price-insensitive customers) would result in competitive advantage for the firm, then it should not be considered as an option.

Characterizing the options as stories helps ensure that they are not seen negatively as "your opinion," "biased," or "unsubstantiated." They are simply ways of thinking about the market that may or may not be proven to have validity. This characterization helps ensure that more radical, out-of-the-box ideas are put on the table and that the goal of inclusiveness is met. There is plenty of time for the process to reduce the option set, but the process will underachieve if the sourcing of options at the front end is restricted.

> The AP management team generated eleven options, then reviewed and synthesized those options into the following five: (1) & (2) forward integration at the existing pulp mill into two different grades of value-added paper; (3) closing of the pulp mill and replacing it with a solid-wood products operation to maintain timber rights; (4) merger with a key West Coast player to simultaneously improve the industry structure and generate a competitively attractive position in combination; and (5) selling off the entire West Coast operations including the pulp mill, sawmills and timber rights. The status quo was rejected as an option because no member of the team could tell a compelling story as to how the status quo could produce competitive advantage.

Specify Conditions

The third step in the process is to specify the key conditions that would need to be substantiated in order for the management team to believe that the story is sound and therefore an option to which they could commit themselves.

We use a process called reverse engineering to identify the key conditions that would have to hold for a given option to be sound. The reverse engineering framework explores conditions in four broad areas of typical relevance to strategy—the industry, customer needs, relative competitive position, competitor response—to identify the conditions that must be satisfied for each option to be sound.

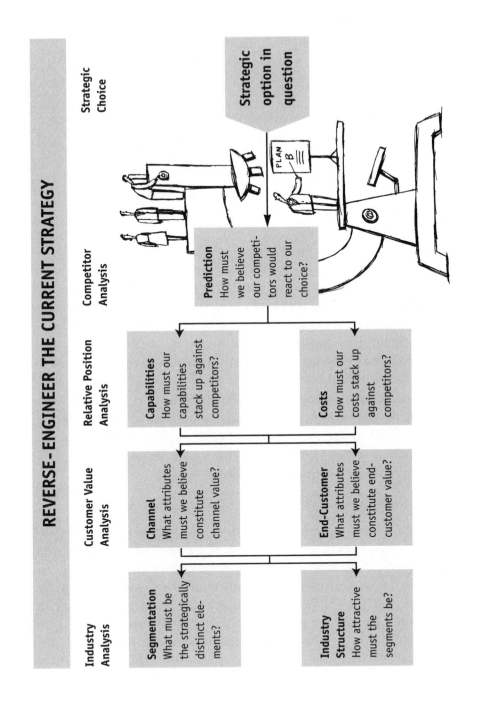

REVERSE-ENGINEER THE CURRENT STRATEGY

| Industry Analysis | Customer Value Analysis | Relative Position Analysis | Competitor Analysis | Strategic Choice |

Strategic option in question

Prediction
How must we believe our competitors would react to our choice?

Capabilities
How must our capabilities stack up against competitors?

Costs
How must our costs stack up against competitors?

Channel
What attributes must we believe constitute channel value?

End-Customer
What attributes must we believe constitute end-customer value?

Segmentation
What must be the strategically distinct elements?

Industry Structure
How attractive must the segments be?

In the case of AP's solid-wood products option, for example: (1) that segments of the solid-wood market are big enough to enable AP to use its timber cutting rights to a sufficient extent to retain them; (2) that these segments are and will continue to be sufficiently structurally attractive to warrant AP's entry; (3) that the specific wood resources AP controls (i.e., tree variety and size) are appropriate for the customers' needs; and (4) that AP can achieve a competitive cost position in the chosen segments.

At this point, the process does not seek to dismiss or even question options. Rather, the process seeks to have those in the management team with reservations about a particular option specify what condition they would need to see met in order to feel confident about the option. Making the origins of these reservations clear will enable each option to be tested in public rather than tested privately in the minds of team members. If the conditions are tested and validated, the public testing will generate commitment to action. If conditions are invalidated, then the generator of the option will see that the option has been fairly considered and found not to have sufficient merit to prevail as the choice.

Prioritize the Barriers to Choice

The fourth step further focuses the resources applied to strategic choice by prioritizing the conditions based on the degree to which they constitute a barrier to choice. In this step the participants analyze the conditions that represent the greatest barriers first, so that other conditions will not have to be explored if the prior barrier is not overcome.

In what we call "the lazy man's approach to strategy," we

analyze the conditions in the reverse order of the management team's confidence that they will be confirmed. In this way, if the condition about which they are least confident cannot be met, none of the remaining conditions will have to be explored.

This sequential approach minimizes the amount of analytical work necessary, which saves both time and resources. For example, we helped one major manufacturer study its choices and reach fundamental conclusions about the future of the business in just 14 weeks.

In the case of the solid-wood option, the management team was least confident of the match of the specific wood resources to market segments that could support the scale of operation required. Thus the exploration of market segment size and match with wood resources came first, and questions of structural attractiveness and cost competitiveness were left for later.

Design Valid Tests

The final step in the choice-structuring process is to build commitment to the choice. For each key barrier condition (in order of the prioritization in Step Four), we work with the management team—member by member as necessary—to specify the test that they would see as compelling in confirming the proposition that the condition holds. Management team members may have different tests that they view as valid, resulting in the need to apply multiple tests for a given condition. However, in practice, management teams tend to be able to coalesce around a single test that they see as valid.

The AP team worked together to design a test for the condition on solid-wood products segment size. They felt that the wood products operation would have to utilize a minimum of 70 percent of the current allowable timber cut for the government not to take back the rights. (The rest could be sold as logs and chips to other mill operators.) They felt that the most new wood products segments (e.g., multi-density fibreboard, kiln-dried dimensional lumber, cedar shakes) AP could comfortably enter would be three distinct product segments (or they would risk being overwhelmed by the complexity of the new operation). They further felt that it would be unreasonable to assume that AP could achieve a market share of the product segment higher than the current North American market share leader. Hence the test was: Could three or fewer product segments in which AP achieved market share equal to the North American share leader utilize at least 70 percent of the current allowable cut?

In addition to having a view on the nature of the test which would confirm the condition in question, each member of the management team will have a standard of proof associated with the condition and the test of that condition. The more skeptical the manager, the higher the burden of proof. In order to build commitment, it is critical to set the standard of proof for each test (and each element of the test) as the standard generated by the most demanding member of the management team. Each manager must specify the standard of proof that would, if achieved in the subsequent testing, cause him/her to be sufficiently confident to be committed to the choice.

Different AP managers had different standards of proof for the wood products segment size test. Some managers felt that 50 or 60 percent utilization of the allowable cut would be sufficient to maintain rights, but one manager felt the standard would be 70 percent. Some managers felt that they could successfully enter numerous segments, but one manager felt that three was the maximum with which he would be comfortable. Some managers felt that it would be possible to enter certain segments and achieve dominant market share, but others felt uncomfortable in using that as an assumption. Hence the test combined the highest standard of proof across the various sub-elements.

The ultimate goal is to design tests that will enable each member of the management team to put his hand on his heart and commit himself to both choosing and taking action on the choice if the analysis confirms the condition. This designs quality into the choice process from the beginning.

The wood products work revealed that indeed there were several segments of the wood products market that were of sufficient size to confirm the first priority test. However, the second test failed to confirm the match between the needs of those segments and the specific wood resources. AP's mix of tree species was not a good match for the product segments (the analysis demonstrated that the segments in question required much more homogenous wood resources in size and species than AP's wood resources). Hence this option was eliminated without performing detailed structural attractiveness or cost competitiveness work.

The wood products option was eliminated, as were the two paper options (due to cost competitiveness and evolving structural attractiveness), and the merger/restructuring option (no potential partner was able to produce the required benefits). Exit was the only remaining option. Despite the challenge in reconciling this option with the overall strategy of the firm, the management team made the choice to exit at the end of the analytical process, and AP announced that its entire West Coast operation was for sale.

1. **The choice is easier to make when the time comes**. Through choice structuring, the team identifies the barriers to choice at the inception of the process rather than at the end of the process. By anticipating these roadblocks and discussing them early, the team has more time to work through critical roadblocks and can avoid spending time and resources on non-critical analyses or analyses with less than compelling standards of proof.

   In addition, the management team builds emotional commitment to what can be a tough choice from the beginning of the process by considering the option and describing what proof would be necessary for them to commit themselves to it. If the analyses come back confirming that pursuing a difficult option is required, the team has already gone through a substantial portion of the difficult emotional work by having considered the option and laid out the conditions at the beginning of the process.

2. **The choice is designed for action.** The choice-structuring process explicitly builds commitment

throughout the process. This is an important benefit because it is difficult and time-consuming to sell the choice to key managers after the fact. Additionally, the process of specifying options and conditions not only allows, but demands, that the management team be specific about the actions and operational implications that would arise from, or be required by, each option, hence speeding the translation of choice into action.

3. **The overall strategy development process is more economic and efficient.** The choice structuring process focuses the expensive and time-consuming data collection and analysis sequentially on only the most critical questions and eliminates extraneous work. Task forces—whether internal or external—will be much more cost-effective if their work is guided by an effective choice-structuring process.

—RM

Author's Note

Martin identifies four attributes of a high quality strategy choice. It is genuine. It must be made between at least two viable options and it must specify what the firm must do or not do. It is sound. The choice flows logically from accumulated facts and figures. It is a well-thought-out choice that does depend minimally on intuition. Nor is it overly influenced by power positions. It is subject to sustained and open testing. The choice is actionable; it specifies the goals and doable tasks required to implement the choice. Finally, the choice is compelling to subordinates and to top management.

With the exception of being compelling, the actions required to meet the other attributes are spelled out in the literature of competitive strategy. Defining options, specifying what is included and excluded, making valid inferences from data, and testing the conclusions rigorously are at the core of the methodologies available for defining competitive strategy. For example, Porter's (1980), five forces is but one concept that can be used to determine the nature of the environment and the analyses required to make sound choices.

Competitive strategy is therefore a theory of action that espouses how to make sound choices and how to test them rigorously. One sign of a sound competitive strategy is that if the specifications are followed correctly, there will be a minimal gap between the espoused theory and the theory-in-use about producing strategic choices. The requirements of competitive strategy are therefore the primary drivers of action on the part of the strategy professionals and line management. To put this another way, the tests for soundness of the choices are derivable from the theory of competitive strategy.

Creating a compelling choice means that it generates management commitment. Part of that commitment is driven by the rigorous logic and testing that has been used in formulating choices. To the extent the commitment is caused by these factors, the commitment of line management is external. They commit to it because of the rigorous analysis.

Martin advises that external commitment is necessary but it is not sufficient. He advises commitment that activates ongoing energy for vigilance in monitoring the effectiveness of the implementation. Internal commitment is produced by using a theory whose basis is not competitive strategy but the production of human enthusiasm, energy, personal responsibility. Model II theories-in-use, Model II social virtues, and a culture with minimal organizational defensive routines are the primary causal factors of internal commitment.

It is probably true that the first three attributes of a high quality choice are not influenced strongly by interpersonal theories of action. True, the users could differ on the meaning of rigor and valid testing. But, for the sake of argument, let us assume that such problems are minimal. Such an assumption is not problematic to our view because, if it were not true, it would simply mean that concepts such as Model II could be introduced earlier in the processes of defining choice.

Summary

Competitive strategy and a theory of action are theories of effective action. They are based on the same governing values of valid information, informed choice, and personal responsibility to monitor the effectiveness of the implementation of choice.

The goal of either theory is to make their respective espoused theories consistent with their theories-in-use. This is accomplished in the case of competitive strategy by teaching the individual the concepts of competitive strategy.

Teaching the theory of action perspective is more complicated. Individuals are skillful at defensive reasoning, self-referential logic, and unilateral control that there is a built-in gap between espoused theory and theory-in-use. There are three sets of causal claims that this theory must meet. The first is the claim that Model I leads to the specified counterproductive consequence and the causal processes by which this occurs. These include the counterproductive consequences that Model I theories-in-use predict will be enacted in organizations (e.g., organizational defensive routines). The second set of causal claims are those related to using Model II theories-in-use and the claims of what will occur if they are used (e.g., reduction of organizational defensive routines). Finally, there is a third set of claims that must be tested that are related to how to move from Model I theories-in-use and social virtues, as well as organizational defensive routines.

The challenge of integrated management and consulting is to integrate requirements of strategic choice and effective action in dealing with human beings. There are, at least, three reasons why we can be optimistic about moving toward effective integration. They are:

1. **Competitive choice and theory of action are both theories of effectiveness**. The former is about producing high-quality choices. The latter is about human relationships that lead to effective leadership, internal commitment, and learning.
2. **Both are theories that are built on the use of productive reasoning**. Both theories are based on accurate description, valid inferences, and robust testing of claims.
3. **Both theories are based on the same governing values.** The values are those consistent with Model II. They are valid information, informed choice, and personal responsibility to monitor vigilantly the validity and effectiveness of the actions based on their respective perspectives.

11

Building Generic Competence in Organizational Learning

AS WE HAVE SEEN IN EARLIER CHAPTERS, building an organization that excels at double-loop learning and one that genuinely integrates the necessary managerial tasks with the relevant human factors is critical. What follows is a plan for creating such an organization—one that engages both the minds and the spirits of the participants.

A plan to create a learning organization should have as its goal integrating business issues with the emotional issues that inevitably arise when people are at work solving complex problems. For example, a program to create a learning organization would include teaching Model II behavior in the context of solving business problems. These problems might include: challenges around competitive strategy, managing information, reducing the rigidity of the stovepipe mentality, improving quality performance, and, of course, detecting and correcting errors wherever they occur.

To be successful, a program to create a learning organization must begin at the top. Learning and behaving in ways consistent with Model II, as we have seen, requires shaking up the status quo and developing new criteria for effectiveness. It also means coming to grips with skilled incompetence, skilled unawareness, fancy footwork, and undiscussables.

The most effective way to champion these Model II skills is for the leaders of any organization to produce them in their dealings with others and their immediate subordinates. In this way, they demonstrate their new skills. And, perhaps more important, they demonstrate that they are willing to be challenged when they are not using Model II skills.

What follows are several guidelines for creating a comprehensive learning program. They flow directly from the theory of action perspective outlined in Chapter 2.

Guidelines for Building a Comprehensive Learning Program

1. Any program intended to produce changes in actual behavior must begin by focusing on the behavior as it is being produced in the everyday life in the organization. This means that the participants must be willing to have their actual behavior observed. The most robust mode is tape-recording the sessions. Next, participants must be willing to be observed by competent outsiders with the hope that as the participants become skillful, they themselves will begin to take on the role of observer.

2. Focusing on these behaviors, however, is not enough. Awareness alone will not get at the causal factors of the behaviors—the theories-in-use, the social virtues, the organizational defensive routines, and the ways in which they interact to produce an ultra-stable state

against double-loop learning. In order to get at these factors, it is necessary for the participants to explore their skilled incompetence, skilled unawareness, and fancy footwork. Such a commitment requires that they will strive to be open, to try not to bypass and cover up these factors, and to commit to having their bypass and cover-ups discussable.

3. In order to make a genuine commitment, the participants will also have to learn to be skillful at productive reasoning and to reduce the use of defensive reasoning.

4. The evidence for the quality and depth of the commitment will come from tape recording actual sessions and "scoring" them as illustrated in the cases that have been described. The focus on tape recordings (or skilled observation) has several important payoffs. First, tape-recording is easy and can be relatively unobtrusive We find that the participants forget the tape recorder if the subject matters they are discussing are crucial and important. If the focus is on routine and not important issues, then the tape recorder can be obtrusive. Second, the tape recorder becomes a trusted vehicle by which the participants can get a better feel for what went on during an important encounter. Tape recorders are not seen as having defenses or axes to grind. Therefore at the outset they are more trustworthy than colleagues who may act as observers. Third, tape recordings provide an opportunity for reflection. Participants may return to the meeting again and again. Fourth, tape recordings provide the most powerful evaluations of theories-in-use, social virtues, and organizational defensive routines. Individuals find reading portions of a transcript

or listening to a portion of a tape a highly compelling evaluative technique. As I have already shown, it is possible for executives to report changes that they honestly believe occurred and be unaware that no changes, in theory-in-use, social virtues, or organizational defensive routines have occurred. Tape recording helps to close that gap. Fifth, it is possible to use the analysis of the tape recordings to redesign change programs in order to make them more powerful. For example, the directors of the consulting firm to be described below found the maps of their defensive routines to be a useful way to organize what they had to change and to measure the extent to which they actually were able to change.

In this chapter, I should like to illustrate how this strategy was, and continues to be, implemented at Monitor Company, a global consulting firm located in Cambridge, Massachusetts. The idea for this program began at the top. The firm was created by a group of individuals all of whom had had previous experience at prestigious consulting firms. These individuals realized the importance of learning as a competency. They also realized that it would be unlikely that they could provide quality advice *and* add value to their clients without becoming a learning organization. In addition, they understood that building these generic competencies had to begin with the leaders of the firm.

The Clients' Presentation of the Problems

The intervention began with the top directors and owners of the consulting firm. These directors feared reproducing in their organization the same factors that led them to leave other consulting firms.* The directors gave many illustrations of their behaviors in meetings to reinforce this fear.

For example, in their meetings the directors felt that people were not candid and that their decision making was not as powerful as possible. They also described rivalries that existed that could split up the firm in ways that would be counter-productive. Indeed, it was not difficult to obtain actual behaviors that illustrated the lack of candidness, the rivalries, and other defenses.

These descriptions were a necessary first step. However, they do not explain why these problems occurred. Employing a theory of action approach, we identified the factors and organized them in a causal array. We then specified how each factor was interdependent with the others and how, in turn, this produced the problems that were counterproductive to the directors' intentions.

In order to organize our explanation, we produced a map that described these factors and their causal relationships. An action map begins by defining the conditions that all the directors agree underlie their values and the way they govern the firm. These "governing conditions" are accepted as "given" by all the directors. For example, all the directors believe that the firm should produce the highest quality of advice and the most value-added performance possible. The directors also expressed a high degree of respect and trust in each other as human beings. They also expressed a low degree of respect and trust in their competence to deal with the different interpersonal issues among themselves.

---

*The case is discussed in detail in my book, *Knowledge for Action* (1993).

The next step was to describe not only the behavior that they reported but also the behavior I observed during the deliberations of the board. For example, the members worked hard to sell their ideas to others, but they did not encourage inquiry into or testing of their ideas. Whenever conflict arose, they tried to smooth it over.

In addition, the directors requested candidness, but since the candid comments were often crafted negatively, the recipients become upset. As a result, discussions about difficult issues often became paralyzed.

Not surprisingly, these actions caused the directors to feel a low degree of confidence in the effectiveness of the group. In addition, these same factors led to mediocre resolution of problems—resolutions that were often based on false consensus. All this, in turn, led the individuals to distance themselves from their own responsibility for error.

Coalition-building, lobbying, horse trading, and empire building were all the rule. Direct or indirect bad-mouthing among directors also occurred. Doubt and cynicism about the group's problem solving and decision making effectiveness developed. However, despite all these tensions, the directors continued to express a high degree of confidence that the firm could produce real value for the client. The map also highlighted difficult and "wicked" problems and "hot" situations that were potentially embarrassing or threatening.

What Does the Map Mean?

The map represents a causal explanation of the problems described by the directors as well as the problems I observed directly. It is an inference and therefore requires testing. There are several ways to test the validity of the map. To begin with, the directors must critique the map. Getting the director's views is important and, as we will see, their views produced corrections.

But this is not the only validation required. The conversation about the map must be tape-recorded, and the quality of the dialogue the directors produce must be consistent with the map. For example, the directors should make evaluations and attributions, and should craft them in ways that are not testable. They should use self-referential logic and defensive reasoning. Even one example to the contrary would jeopardize the causal claims hypothesized because individuals with Model I theories-in-use will continue to produce Model I actions and consequences, even though they now realize that these theories-in-use are a causal factor.

Similarly, the tape recordings must be analyzed to see the extent to which the directors act to create self-fueling counterproductive processes. Again, one episode to the contrary places the hypothesis in doubt.

The testing provides a basis for assessing the validity of the theory being used, and it provides a genuine opportunity for the directors to disagree with the conclusions. However, if the map proves reliable, the directors are responsible for their actions. They cannot squirm out of their personal responsibility with some fancy footwork. Indeed, the fancy footwork would only provide further evidence of their defenses.

The Critique

When shown the map, the CEO said that although he agreed with it, he could not see how he would change his actions when he returned to the office. Fair enough since understanding is not enough to change behaviors. I then introduced the group to Models I and II social virtues, and to organizational defensive routines. With the help of the map that they had just validated, I also illustrated such concepts as skilled incompetence and skilled unawareness.

I then made another prediction. Even though they agreed to the validity of the map, even though they agreed to meet again to begin working on their theories-in-use, and even though they learned about Model II, they would not be able to change the map and the ultra-stable state it depicted between now and the next scheduled session.

Several months went by before the next session. As I predicted, the directors' organizational defenses continued with only one observable difference. Once in a while the directors would reflect on their own or others' actions. (e.g., untested attributions) and identify them. Typically, there would be a smile and recognition, but no further change.

Summary of the First Seminar

Because a detailed description of the first seminar exists (Argyris 1993) I will describe the topics discussed only to show that the discussions were rich with topics previously not discussable. The topics can be grouped into two broad categories. The first concerns the characteristics of the defensive, limited-learning organizational pattern and their interrelationships. It includes the following:

Undiscussable Attributions

- Feeling plain ordinary fear of confrontation
- Thinking it is okay to have limited-learning systems and the politics that go with them
- Using a siege mentality to protect oneself
- Putting down clients

- Using technical knowledge to overpower
- Examining what it means to be a director
- Building coalitions, distancing by the CEO, and covering up both actions
- Describing the reciprocal distancing
- Haggling over who gets the credit
- Perceiving client leads to be allocated in accordance with secret rules and friendships
- Needing to be strong by never asking for help

Self-fulfilling and Self-sealing Consequences

- The CEO feels double binds, bypasses, cover-ups, and becomes upset, all of which leads him to act like a "blast furnace." The other directors cover up their feelings; hence, these processes become undiscussable.
- Directors create discussions that are not helpful and then assign responsibility to the CEO to take action. They condemn him for taking unilateral action.
- Directors engage in distancing, which leads to more distancing and an increased likelihood that distancing is not discussable and hence is self-sealing.
- Directors all feel victimized by a system they created.

The second category includes topics that show the directors reflecting on the total pattern as well as on its implications.

Multiple Causality and Circularity

- Individuals cover up, and the pattern rewards such actions. There is a circular relationship between individuals' responsibility for dysfunctional behavior and the pattern's rewarding such behavior.

- The tension is caused by wicked problems and by failure to deal with fear, embarrassment, or the sense of being threatened in the presence of these problems.

The Next Step

As the members discussed the pattern, several things began to occur that provided important foundations for change. First, the directors confirmed that they made negative attributions about each other and that they did not test or encourage others to test these attributions. The apparent ease and candor with which they admitted their attributions provided evidence that the directors' intentions were not as nasty as the directors themselves evaluated them to be. Moreover, the directors appeared more capable of discussing the undiscussable topics than they had originally thought they would be.

The very act of a thoughtful, spirited inquiry about the action map, in the context of a feedback session managed by an intervenor, provided initial evidence that the overprotective features described in the map were valid but alterable. As a result, the directors became optimistic about changing what they had feared was unchangeable.

At the end of the session, all the directors expressed enthusiasm and a cautiously optimistic prognosis for change. There were at least two reasons why the optimism was cautious. First, many directors wondered what would happen after they left the room and especially what would happen when they returned to the pressures of everyday life. Second, as the intervenor pointed out, for the optimism to become credible, new actions would have to develop and persist. In his opinion, the directors did not have the skills to produce the new actions even though they now wanted to do so.

The intervenor recommended a second seminar to examine the generic action strategies and the theories-in-use that produced them, to learn theories of action that could lead to more productive actions, to practice enacting these espoused theories so that they became a new theory-in-use, and to explore the organizational changes that the new theory-in-use could create. The directors agreed to hold this seminar.

The Second Seminar

Each director completed a case that was discussed by the directors as a group. They acted as consultants to each other. All the cases illustrated features of Model I that we have described in several previous chapters. We will summarize how the cases and their discussion confirmed features of the action map presented earlier.

Action Strategies

The action strategies in the cases were consistent with Model I. For example, whenever the writers attempted to explain another person's intentions, the following actions were apparent:

- Negative attributions were made about the other's intentions and defensiveness.
- Attributions were not tested publicly.
- Negative evaluations were made about the other's performance.
- Evaluations were not tested publicly.

- The stated reason for avoiding testing was that the writer was showing concern for the other.

Coverups

The cases' left-hand columns contained the writers' attributions and evaluations of the CEO, other directors, and clients. They were not communicated to the other person in the conversation, yet these thoughts and feelings were crucial to the way each writer developed his or her strategies and produced his or her conversation.

Limited Learning

There was no reflection on or discussion of the critical issues that were being covered up. Moreover, each case showed that the writer protected himself, that the writer believed the CEO protected himself, and that underlying issues in the resource allocation system were never discussed.

Self-fulfilling and Self-sealing Processes

The case writers found serious faults with the allocation system and with the CEO's behavior. They entered into the dialogue with doubts that the basic problems would be resolved. The way they crafted their conversations and censored them to cover up their thoughts and feelings made it likely that the problems identified in the cases would not be resolved by those conversations. Moreover, given the undiscussability of the left-hand columns and the Model I crafting of the conversation, it was unlikely that the parties would see that they were responsible for creating self-fulfilling processes as well as conditions under which these processes would not be discussed. Hence, their action strategies led to processes that sealed the dysfunctional processes, and these self-sealing processes were not discussed.

Analysis of the Discussion of the Cases

All the dysfunction apparent in the cases should be expected to lead to the sense of helplessness and the distancing identified in the map. Indeed, these consequences were actually produced during the discussion of the cases in the two-day change seminar. Here are some telling episodes from that discussion:

> **Larry*:** My attitude in this conversation and in the thirty-five times that I have had it in the last two years is not that the CEO obstructs the solution. It is that there is literally no solution.
>
> **CEO:** Yes, I agree with the conversation in the case. My thoughts and feelings were something along the lines of "Why are we bothering to have a conversation about something there is no decent answer to? We can solve 50 percent of this problem, but I wonder if we are going to talk about the 50 percent for which there is no answer."

Several directors openly confirmed their sense of hopelessness. They also admitted that the only strategy left for them was to deal with the CEO individually and to hold him responsible for solving the problem. They said they asked for more resources than they expect to get and they act as if this were

---

*The names used are not their real names.

not the case. The CEO, on the other hand, sensed this but covered up his views.

> **CEO:** My left-hand column is that I will probably be asked to give each of you the eighteen people whose names you've written down.
>
> (Later) I feel our discussions are useless because there is no flexibility on your part.
>
> (Later) Everyone tends to use overly dramatic statements; therefore, I have to discount what you say and, of course, act as if I am not doing so.
>
> **David:** (Tells the CEO that he does not realize how he causes the very problems that he wants to solve.)
>
> **CEO:** (disagrees that he causes the problems) If you all agree that we have too few people, then the majority of the problems are created by you fellows. Why can't you guys manage yourselves?
>
> **David:** The problem is that each of us has different views of the rules.
>
> **CEO:** I don't believe that. I have resisted exerting coercive power over you. You are allegedly both adults and my partners. I will never order you to do these things. If you want me [to become coercive], then you can have my letter of resignation.
>
> **Larry:** What is the nature of the compensation scheme? On what basis are we rewarded?
>
> **CEO:** I do run the compensation scheme as a political process in order to keep the coalition together. I have had the belief that some of these undiscussable issues would cause so much upheaval that I have deliberately made things

vague. The alternative would be collective discussability, which I have always thought would be too disruptive.

Jim: Compensation that is dollars is a minority issue. The issue is self-worth and relative worth. We shouldn't kid ourselves.

Several directors: (They discuss Jim, who brings more business to the firm than the others do. Some see him as arrogant and self-centered; others are annoyed because they believe he is getting most of the human resources, as well as keeping the best clients. The discussion is candid on all sides.)

Jim: (says he feels he is in a bind) If I get the business, I am damned; if I did not get it, I would be damned. I work my butt off for the firm [and I am not appreciated].

John: I suspect that all of us envy you, and those feelings get in the way.

Signs of Learning

As the two-day seminar progressed, apparently inconsistent actions were observed. While most of the actions were guided by Model I theory-in-use, others, often little ones, suggested that Model II theory-in-use was being learned. (This imbalance of Model I over Model II is typical of most sessions during the early stages of intervention.)

The comments reproduced above were taken from a discussion of an evaluation of a senior consultant. Some directors felt the case was not one from which they could learn. They made attributions that the writer chose the case in order to bypass difficult issues about his performance and to look good. The conversation is scored to show which actions are characteristic of Model I.

WHAT WAS SAID	SCORING THE CONVERSATION
Jim: I find this case interesting, but not very useful for our learning.	**Advocacy:** no illustration, no inquiry, no testing
Bill: Well, I checked it out with Chris (the intervenor).	
Jim: My left-hand side (i.e., his uncensored thought) in reading the case is that you picked a bunny.	
Ted: I had the identical reaction. I thought it was the ultimate safe topic.	**Evaluation:** no inquiry, no illustration, no testing
David: I strongly disagree.	**Advocacy:** no illustration no inquiry, no testing
Jim: Another left-hand attribution is that you resent being described as mushy or soft or chicken, and you wrote the case to prove you are none of these.	**Attribution:** no illustration, no inquiry, no testing
David: It does not surprise me at all that he wrote this case because it is a tough one, politically speaking, in the firm and the guy he wrote about is his friend.	**Attribution:** no inquiry, partial illustration, no testing
Larry: I think that Bill is trying to learn not to be mushy.	**Attribution and evaluation:** no inquiry, no illustration, no testing
Bill: What do you think would have been a more appropriate case for me to write?	

Jim: (Answers with an example.)

Bill: I didn't remember that incident.

Jim: My attribution is that (when you raise these issues) it takes the form of "Doctor, I have a friend who has a problem." My read of your tone is that (you are saying to the individual in the case) "I have a problem with your behavior. I have a lot of anxiety about you." As I read it, my left-hand column was screaming, "This is a cop-out."

Evaluation: no illustration, no inquiry, no testing

Evaluation: no illustration, no inquiry, no testing

Evaluation: no illustration, no inquiry, no testing

Bill: I agree with the first part but not with the second. I believe you are wrong.

Evaluation: no illustration, no inquiry, no testing

Larry: My impression of this discussion is that we are exorcising ghosts again. It's not the reality today. We are focusing on ancient concerns.

Embedded in this primarily Model I dialogue were signs of learning. For example, Jim raised doubts about the value the case had for learning, and several directors described the use of "bunny" cases because a norm was developing that such cases did not provide much food for learning.

Individuals were beginning to make public their uncensored or left-hand-column thoughts, noting that before this seminar the thoughts would have remained censored. Bill appeared to look for an example of an attribution when he asked the others what case they thought would have been appropriate. Later Jim began to use the concept of attribution, and he also revealed his feelings about Bill's tone in the case and his anxiety that Bill was copping out.

Finally, Larry stated that the discussion was focused on "ancient concerns." This eventually led to a discussion of how the case might represent current issues. The session concluded with the directors evaluating it positively. They acknowledged that they had a long way to go to develop the competency that they desired. Indeed, several said that they now realized that this program was truly continuous and probably never ending. They concluded by committing energy, time, and resources to continue the program.

Conducting Learning Experiments

In the next phase, each director planned his own follow-up sessions. Each selected a problem that not only was important to him but that called for skills that, if he could develop them, would be applicable to many further problems. These sessions were also tape-recorded for research and educational purposes. The recordings were used to analyze the progress the directors were making or the lack thereof. The directors used the recordings to reflect on their learning and to further develop their skills.

The problems the directors selected represented crucial challenges to their skills and continued their learning. For example, two directors examined their mistrust of each other. Another director questioned the underlying commitment of the CEO to his role in the firm. The directors examined the meaning of being an owner, and the CEO developed a new ownership plan that the directors approved. The directors then held a group evaluation of the CEO's performance. Two directors, each of whom believed they were being undermined by the other, resolved the problem.

An analysis of the tape recordings from this session indicates that the directors have continued to expand their range of competence to produce Model II conversations, although Model I has by no means disappeared.

The intervention is now being expanded in several directions. First, sessions similar to the first ones in which the directors participated are being offered throughout the organization. Second, concepts of Model II inquiry and learning are being integrated into the education of senior consultants and case team managers. Third, a group of consultants who can become the internal change agents and educators for the firm is being developed. Finally, there has been an expansion of the intervention into the firm's client relationships. For example, the firm is using action maps to describe important features of the behavioral worlds of the client organizations. The firm is also developing ways to produce maps that genuinely integrate behavioral features with technical features. Several directors have designed and implemented with senior clients change programs similar to the one they experienced.

12

Summary

THIS SUMMARY IS ORGANIZED in two parts. Part I summarizes my main conclusions regarding producing actionable knowledge for any discipline. This is followed with a summary regarding producing actionable knowledge for the human resources activities that are the focus of this book. Part II includes a new example that illustrates a concern I have around a relatively new kind of focus in the business literature—that is, the exultation of best practice—which in this case takes the form of something called the successful company syndrome. Let me begin by summarizing our work to date.

Requirements for Crafting Actionable Knowledge for Any Discipline

In order for advice from practitioners or for propositions from scholars to be actionable, they must be crafted in ways that

238

the human mind can reproduce them. This means that advice or propositions should stipulate the following:

- The theories-in-use that specify the sequence of behaviors required to produce the intended consequences or goals.
- The theories-in-use should be crafted in ways that make the causality transparent.
- The causality embedded in the theories-in-use is testable robustly in the context of everyday life.
- Actionable knowledge must specify the values that underlie and govern the designs-in-use.

These requirements should hold for any activity. For example, accounting rules specify how to diagnose cost drivers. The specifications meet the requirements of a theory in use because they state the behavioral sequences required to produce a cost-driven analysis and ways to test the validity of the results. If two individuals are given the same numbers and come up with different numerical conclusions, then an error has been made. However, it is possible to review the actions of each individual to locate the disconnect and to correct it. All this can be done because the causal specifications for producing cost drivers are transparent and testable.

Managerial professional disciplines are, in effect, theories of action. Each contains espoused theories and theories-in-use. The aspiration is to minimize recognized or unrecognized gaps and inconsistencies between the espoused designs and the designs-in-use. This aspiration is taken seriously in the professions. In many cases, they require practitioners, such as accountants, to pass certification tests that indicate they are competent to produce the service that they claim they can produce. This is not to say the gaps and inconsistencies may not exist. It is to say that the professionals strive continuously to surface and minimize them.

Requirements for Crafting Actionable Knowledge In Human Resources Activities That Are the Focus of This Book

We have found that human beings learn theories of effective action early in their lives. On the basis of our research, we state that the overwhelming number of human beings are acculturated to a Model I theory-in-use.

We have also found systematic gaps and inconsistencies between the espoused theory and the theory-in-use. We know that individuals are systematically unaware of the gaps as they produce them. If they are aware, they hold factors outside themselves to be responsible for the gaps and inconsistencies.

These problems are caused by skillful use of Model I and the defensive reasoning on which it is based. Hence, unawareness and incompetence are due to skill, not the lack of it. Also, Model I theories-in-use produce organizational defensive routines and make them undiscussable, and the undiscussability non-discussable. The result is a systematic, self-fueling set of actions that inhibit learning, especially double-loop learning— precisely when it is needed the most.

It is fair to claim that if we analyze carefully the advice described in Part I, the overwhelming amount seeks to create conditions at the individual, small group, intergroup, and organizational levels that is consistent with Model II. However although the advisors espouse Model II, their theory-in-use is

Model I. Consistent with Model I, the advisors are unaware of the gaps. When they discover gaps, they hold others responsible. This is why Tom preached Model II theories-in-use, but acted consistently with Model I when he got into difficulties with the line managers. This also explains why the change professionals criticized Tom for his inconsistencies. When asked to produce helpful advice, it was abstract and not producible. Moreover, when we analyzed the tape recordings of the advice they gave Tom, it contained all the inconsistencies and gaps that Tom used and that they were advising him not to use. Change professionals may espouse actions consistent with Model II, but their theory-in-use when they take action is Model I.

The Success Syndrome

A significant part of today's business literature now deals exclusively with success stories and as a result the study of "best practices" has become a genre in its own right. Much can be learned from studying success, of course. However, it is necessary to understand clearly the roots of that success in order to draw the correct lessons from it.

Mark Twain once said that a cat that jumps on a hot stove never does it again. But then again, he also tells us, that cat never jumps on a cold stove either. Success, then, can breed conservatism, which in a fast-changing, competitive environment can cause failure—but is it inevitably so?

Two senior members of the Delta Consulting Group believe so. After spending some time studying their clients businesses, they believe that a company's sustained success inevitably carries the seeds of future disasters (Nadler and

Nadler 1998, p. 1). In order for this claim to lead to valid recommendations and actions to solve this dilemma, it is necessary that the following questions be answered:

- How is sustained success defined and measured?
- What behavioral mechanism causes the seeds of future
  disaster?
- What behavioral mechanism causes the future disaster
  to be inevitable?

Let us assume that the organizations that the authors use to
illustrate their findings are indeed examples of successful
organizations with dominant market positions. I ask the
reader to accept this assumption because I believe their claim
applies to more than successful organizations that have a history of dominance. Their findings apply to organizations that
do not dominate and are in the state of some degree of failure.
The more fundamental error made by the authors is that they
have excluded a range of other companies. This error is non-
trivial for the executives who may conclude wrongly that the
findings do not apply to them, thereby missing an opportunity to correct any failures in their organizations.

The authors specify a series of interrelated causal claims
about the success syndrome and its consequences. Briefly,
they are:

- When organizations are successful and dominant, they
  become convinced that they are right. This, in turn,
  causes them to stop paying attention to important
  changes in the external world.
- According to the authors, it follows that the organiza-

tions assume that they have nothing to fear or learn from their competitors. They also reject ideas and strategies that are not homegrown. A not-invented-here syndrome takes over.

- It follows that whatever processes get associated with success become formalized, inflexible policies and procedures.
- It follows that as more practices become codified, complexity increases dramatically.
- It follows that risk is discouraged and conservatism grows.
- It follows that learning is disabled and innovation reduced.
- It follows that, over time, the above lead to increased costs, loss of speed, and impaired capacity to act.

This causal scenario appears sensible and it is illustrated by many examples. If so, what is the problem?

In order for these causal claims to be validated, the authors would have to specify the actual behavioral mechanisms that cause people to act consistently with the causal scenario above. There are at least two reasons for this requirement. (1) Knowing the causality explicitly is key for designing interventions. (2) If the causal mechanisms are made explicit, we may learn that the scenario is valid for organizations with moderate to low success and that do not dominate their markets. If this is true, then the authors have a theory that is comprehensive. And, if it is comprehensive, then the causes and the change programs would be the same for all organizations.

The authors claim that one of the pervasive causes of the successful company syndrome is that the activities become routinized and inflexible. Inflexibility is a key variable in their analysis. Yet the causal mechanisms of inflexibility are not made explicit. All we get is the abstract scenario described above.

The authors' recommendations assume that organizational inflexibility can be reduced significantly if the executives follow the consultant's advice. How do they know that this is likely? If organizations with failure syndrome (of varying degrees) are also inflexible and resistant to learning; if they discourage risk taking, encourage conservatism, create unnecessary costs, could there be a more fundamental set of causes operating?

The framework of defensive reasoning and organizational defensive routines described in Part II provides a possible answer. In order to introduce it, I should like to begin with some observations that are known by the authors.

In the companies identified by the authors, there were individuals who saw that the features of the Success Syndrome were operating. They often advised against ignoring it. Many of those individuals reported that they were unsuccessful in creating a drive for change. Moreover, many reported that they were often discouraged by those colleagues who assured them that things were not as bad as they suggested. They were also advised to be careful lest they develop a reputation for being negative.

According to our framework, a key causal factor was that these issues were undiscussable and their undiscussability was undiscussable. This leads to an examination of the organizational defensive routines and the defensive reasoning used by the players. It is possible that it is the defensive reasoning and the organizational defensive routines that are causally responsible for the scenarios of the Success Syndrome. If so, then using the Success Syndrome as the explanation is incorrect. It is not success that causes internal focus, rigidity, inflexibility, and conservation. It is the undiscussability of these and other factors that create the seeds for disaster. But they do so for all companies.

The authors' explanation leads them to advise practitioners to avoid the Success Syndrome in ways that can be misleading. For example, the CEOs should demonstrate by their own behaviors that an external focus is important. This isn't simply a matter of broadcasting. The CEOs must pay concrete, ongoing attention. The authors report that David Kearns of Xerox got the attention of inwardly focused executives by ordering them to work in customer service centers. I agree that this type of action should help. But it bypasses the important question of why this action was needed in the first place. It bypasses the defensive reasoning and the organizational defenses that caused the executives to be myopic and the organizational defensive routines that rewarded the myopia.

The same is true for Sun Microsystem's Scott McNealy's reasoning that one of his major responsibilities is to keep worrying about the next big thing. His statement that he is not paid to feel good raises the question about whether he expects his immediate reports to exhibit the same commitment. If so and McNealy has gotten his subordinates to think and feel as he does, how did he do it?

The recommendations given and the consequences promised by the authors are devoid of advice about how to deal with resistance—either overt or covert. For example, it makes sense to tell all the players that their competition could be both right and competent. How is the executive to deal with those subordinates who do not see the validity of such a position? More important, McNealy may find it useful to ask why the executives think this way in the first place. Myopia that is assumed to be valid and rewarded is based on defensive reasoning and protected by organizational defensive routines. Executives who do not discuss this possibility are also using defensive reasoning and reinforcing the organizational defensive routines.

There is another problem with the recommendations that is not addressed by the authors. They recommend that executives should anticipate change by the use of periodic scans of the environment; that they should not wait until a crises occurs; that they should pay attention to the observations of front-line employees. Indeed, are they not obvious? The authors could respond that they may be obvious; indeed, many may espouse them, but they are not part of their theories-in-use. If this is true, and I think that it probably is, then why is it so? Solving this problem is fundamental because it prevents the problems that the authors address.

Leadership and Learning: An Unclear Guide to the Gurus

A recent book called *The Guru Guide* reviews the literature about leadership written by many famous experts and scholars. The authors (Boyett and Boyett 1998) describe the main ideas of each guru in valid ways. They point out that the research results vary widely and that there is much disagreement among the "gurus." Furthermore, the authors conclude that the leadership characteristics described by each guru may be true some of the time, none of the time, or most of the time. In other words, after decades of research, it is difficult to make true and actionable generalizations about leadership. One reason, I suggest, is that most of the scholars focused on describing leadership. These descriptions are abstract and disconnected from everyday practice. They are therefore difficult to test in ways that help to rule out competing ideas.

More important, I suggest, the scholars quoted have given little to no attention to how to *create* the leadership characteristics that they espouse. Thus, the most robust test is rarely if ever taken. By the way, if the scholars specified how to create the features they claim are valid, we would have the basis for designing and implementing interventions to enhance leadership effectiveness.

In the end, the authors ask which of the gurus presents the most compelling view and end up choosing Peter Drucker. Drucker's contention is that effective leaders varied widely in how they behaved and that there was therefore no generalizable personality, style, or trait attached to leadership.

Thus, after decades of research, when two authors try to choose the most effective leadership theories, they select someone who believes that there are no generalizable leadership traits to be found. Drucker may or may not be right; the point is that decades of leadership research has not helped thoughtful writers and practitioners make choices with any certainty of their validity.

I believe, and have tried to illustrate the reasoning behind this belief, that the methodologies used to study leadership focus primarily on producing generalizations that describe it. They do not tell us much about how to create effective leadership. To my knowledge, the one exception is the early work of Kurt Lewin and his associates. The irony is that one of his coworkers, who lauded the early work, attempted to build upon it in order to develop more rigorous conclusions. An analysis of that research suggests that as his research became more rigorous it also became more distant from reality and less actionable (Argyris 1980).

Validity cannot be separated from actionability nor actionability from validity. Only when attention is focused equally on the two, will we have the foundations for overcoming the problems described in this book.

Bibliography

Adler, Paul S. (1993). "Time-and-Motion Regained." *Harvard Business Review* (Jan–Feb): 97–108.

Argyris, C. (1997). "Field Theory as a Basis for Scholarly Research-Consulting." Kurt Lewin Award—Society for the Psychological Study of Social Sciences. *Journal of Social Issues*, 53, (4): 809–824.

Argyris, C. (1996a). "Actionable Knowledge: Design Causality in The Service of Consequential Theory." *Journal of Applied Behavioral Science*, 32 (4): 390–406.

Argyris, C. (1996b). "On Actionable Knowledge." *Journal of Applied Behavioral Science*, 32 (4): 390–406.

Argyris, C. (1996c). "Unrecognized Defenses Of Scholars: Impact on Theory and Research." *Organization Science*, 7 (1): 79–87.

Argyris, C. (1994). "Good Communication that Blocks Learning." *Harvard Business Review*, 72 (4): 77–85.

Argyris, C. (1993). *Knowledge for Action*. San Francisco: Jossey-Bass.

Argyris, C. (1991). "Teaching Smart People How to Learn." *Harvard Business Review*, 69 (3): 99–109.

Argyris, C. (1990a). *Overcoming Organizational Defenses*. Needham, MA: Allyn & Bacon.

Argyris, C. (1990b). "Inappropriate Defenses Against the Monitoring of Organizational Development Practice." *Journal of Applied Behavioral Science*, 26 (3): 299–312.

Argyris, C. (1989). "Strategy Implementation: An Experiment in Learning." New York: American Management Association, *Organizational Dynamics*, August.

Argyris, C. (1987). "Reasoning Action Strategies and Defensive Routines: The Case of OD Practitioners." In Woodman, R.W. and Pas-more, W. A., (eds.), *Research in Organizational Change and Development*, vol. 1. Greenwich, CT: JAI Press, pp. 89–128.

Argyris, C. (1985). *Strategy Change and Defensive Routines*. Boston: Pitman.

Argyris, C. (1982). *Reasoning Learning and Action*. San Francisco: Jossey-Bass.

Argyris, C. (1980). *Inner Contradictions of Rigorous Research*. San Diego, CA: Academic Press.

Argyris, C. and Kaplan, R. S. (1994). "Implementing New Knowledge: The Case of Activity Based Costing." *Accounting Horizons*, 8 (3): 83–105.

Argyris, C., Putnam, R. and Smith, D. (1985). *Action Science*. San Francisco: Jossey-Bass.

Argyris, C. and Schön, D. (1996). *Organizational Learning II*. Reading, MA: Addison-Wesley.

Argyris, C. and Schön, D. (1974). *Theory in Practice*, San Francisco: Jossey-Bass.

Ascari, A., Rock, M. and Dutta, S. (1995). "Re-engineering and Organizational Change: Lessons from a Comparative Analysis of Company Experiences." *European Management Journal*, 13 (1): 1–13.

Barua, A. and Whinston, A. B. (1997). "Getting the Most Out of Re-engineering." *Strategy and Businesses* (7): 13–17.

Bauman, R. P., Jackson, P., and Laurence, J. T. (1997). *From Promise to Performance*. Cambridge, MA: Harvard Business School Press.

Becker, B. and Gerhart, B. (1996). "The Impact of Human Resource Management Organizational Performance: Progress and Prospects." *Academy of Management Journal*, 13 (1): 91–98.

Bowman, C. (1995). "Strategy Workshops and Top-Team Commitment to Strategic Change," *Journal of Managerial Psychology*, 10 (9): 4–12.

Boyett, J. and Boyett, J. (1998). *The Guru Guide*. New York: Wiley.

Burns, T. and Stalker, G. M. (1961). *The Management of Innovation*. London: Tavistock.

Clemons, E. K., Row, M. C., and Thatcher, M. E. (1995). "Identifying Sources of Re-engineering Failures: A Study of the Behavioral Factors Contributing to Re-engineering Risks." *Journal of Management Information Systems*, 12 (2): 9–36.

Covey, S. R. (1989). *The Seven Habits of Highly Effective People*. New York: Simon & Schuster.

De Cock, C. and Hipking, I. (1997). "TQM and BPR: Beyond the Beyond Myth." *Journal of Management Studies*, 34 (5): 659–677.

Doyle, M. and Strauss, D. (1982). *How to Make Meetings Work*. New York: Jove Books.

Eccles, T. (1993). "The Deceptive Allure of Empowerment." *Long Range Planning*, 26 (6): 13–21.

Fitgerald, C. and Kirby, L. K. (1997). *Developing Leaders: Research and Applications in Psychological Type and Leadership Development*. Palo Alto, CA: Davies-Black.

Ford, R. C. and Fottler, M. D. (1995). "Empowerment: A Matter of Degree." *Executive*, 9 (3): 21–29.

Garvin, D. A. (1995). "Leveraged Process for Strategic Advantage." *Harvard Business Review*, (Sept.–Oct.): 77–90.

George, S. (1997). *Uncommon Sense*. New York: Wiley.

Grint, P. and Case, P. (1998) "The Violent Rhetoric of Re-engineering: Management Consulting on the Offensive." *Journal of Management Studies*, 35 (5): 557–578.

Hackman, R. J. and Wageman, R. (1995). "Total Quality Management: Empirical, Conceptual, and Practical Issues." *Administrative Science Quarterly*, 40 (2): 309–342.

Heller, F., Pusic, E., Strauss, G. and Wilpert, B. (1998). *Organizational Participation: Myth and Reality*, Oxford: Oxford University Press.

Hendry, J. (1995). "Processing Re-engineering and the Dynamic Balance of the Organization." *European Management Journal*, 13 (1): 52–57.

Hiltrop, J. M., Despres, C., and Sparrow, P. (1995). "The Changing Role of HR Managers in Europe." *European Management Journal*, 13 (1): 91–98.

Horton, T. R. (1986). *What Works for Me*, New York: Random House Business Division.

Institute of Management. (1996). *Striking the Shackles*, London: GHN Ltd.

Jackson, B. G. (1996). "Re-engineering the Sense of Self: The Managers and the Management Gurus." *Journal of Management Studies*, 33 (5): 571–590.

Johnson, G. (1987). *Strategic Change and the Management Process*, Oxford: Basil Blackwell.

Kaplan, R. S. and Norton, D. P. (1996). *The Balanced Score Card*. Cambridge, MA: Harvard Business School Press.

Katzenback, J. R. and the RCL Team (1995). *Real Change Leaders*. New York: Random House.

Kesler, G. C. (1995). "A Model and Process for Redesigning the HRM Role, in Competencies, and Work in a Major Multi-national Corporation." *Human Resource Management*, 32 (2): 229–252.

Knights, D. and McCabe, D. (1997). "How Would You Measure Something Like That?" *Journal of Management Studies*, 34 (3): 371–388.

Kotter, J. P. (1996). *Leading Change*. Cambridge, MA: Harvard Business School Press.

Lawler, Edward E., III. (1996). *From the Ground Up*. San Francisco: Jossey-Bass.

Legge, K. (1995). *Human Resource Management: Rhetoric and Realities*. Basingstoke: Macmillan.

Lombardo, M. and Eickinger, R. W. (1997). "Human Resources in Building Competitive Edge Leaders." In Ulrich, D., Losey, M. R. and Lake G., (eds.), *Tomorrow's Human Resource Management*. New York: Wiley.

Loyder, M. and Hartley, N. (1995). *Tomorrow's Company*. London: Royal Society for the Encouragement of Arts, Manufacturers and Commerce.

Mazen, A. M. (1997). "Learned Defensiveness: A Neglected Root Cause." *Quality Management Journal*, 4 (2): 24-50.

Meyer, J. P. and Allen, Natalie J. (1997). *Commitment in the Workplace*. Thousand Oaks, CA: Sage.

Mohrman, S. A., Galbraith, J. R., Lawler, Edward E., III. (1998). *Tomorrow's Organization*. San Francisco: Jossey-Bass.

Murphy, K. R. and Cleveland, J. N. (1995). *Understanding Performance Appraisal*, Thousand Oaks: Sage.

Nadler, D. A. and Nadler, B. N. (1998). "The Success Syndrome." N.Y. Drucker Foundation Magazine, Leader to Leader and Executive Forum, Delta Group 7, 1998, pages 1-8.

Porter, M. E. (1980). *Competitive Strategy*. New York: Free Press.

Rymmler, G. A. and Bracke, A. P. (1990). *Improving Performance: How to Manage the White Space in the Organization Chart*. San Francisco: Jossey-Bass.

Schuler, H., Farr, J. L., and Smith, M. (1993). *Personnel Selection and Assessment: Individual and Organizational Perspectives*. Hillsdale, NJ: Lawrence Erlbaum.

Schuler, R. S. (1992). "Strategic human resource management: linking the people with the strategic needs of the business," *Organizational Dynamics*, 21, 1, 18, 32.

Schuler, R. S. (1987). *Personnel and Human Resources Manage-ment*. New York: West Publishing.

Sitken, S. B., Sutclifffe, K. M. and Schroeder, R. G. (1994). "Distin-guishing Control from Learning in Total Quality Management: A Contingency Perspective." *Academy of Management Review*, 19 (3): 537–564.

Smith, D. K. (1996). *Taking Charge of Change*. Reading, MA: Addi-son-Wesley.

Sparrow, P., Schuler, R. S., and Jackson, S. E. (1994). "Convergence or Divergence: Human Resources Practices and Policies for Competitive Advantage Worldwide." *International Journal of Human Resource Management*, 5 (2): 267–299.

Stoddard, D. B., Jarvenpaa, S. L., and Litttlejohn, M. (1996). "The Reality of Business Re-engineering." *California Management Review*, 38 (3): 57–76.

Taylor, J. R. and Van Every, E. J. (1994). *The Vulnerable Fortress*. Toronto: University of Toronto Press.

Ulrich, D. (1997). *Human Resource Champions: The Next Agenda for Adding Value and Delivering Results*. Cambridge, MA: Harvard Business School Press.

Ulrich, D. and Eichinger, R. (1996). *State of the Art (SOTA) Study*. Palm Desert: Commitment for the Human Resource Planning Society.

Ulrich D., Losey, M. R. and Lake, G. (eds.). (1997). *Tomorrow's HR Management*. New York: John Wiley.

Weiss, T. B. and Hartle, F. (1997). Reengineering Performance Man-agement: Breakthroughs in Achieving Strategies Through Peo-ple. Boca Raton, FL: St. Lucie Press.

White, O. F. and Wolf, J. F. (1995). "Demings' Total Quality Manage-ment Movement and the Baskin-Robbins Problem." *Adminis-tration and Society*, 27 (2): 203–225.

Wilkinson, A. (1998). "Empowerment: Theory and Practice." *Per-sonnel Review*, 27 (1): 40–56.

Index

Abstraction, and legitimate technical rating, 114, 117
Action(s): causal claim for, 52; designed, 4, 81; good design as basis for effective, 53; identifying causes for group, 150; self-protective, 150; unforeseen, 143; voting through, 185. *See also* Corrective action; Effective action
Actionability, validity and, 249
Actionable choice, 196
Actionable knowledge: crafting, 238–40; requirements of, 239
Actionable theory, lack of, 90
Action map, 223; inquiry re., 228; use of, 237
Action strategies, 229–30; CIO's, 59; IT group, 60; Model I, 62–63; self-reinforcing pattern of, 60
Adler, Paul S., 45
Advice: as causal, 95–96; characteristics of helpful, 9; critiquing, 99–112; and self-referential logic, 95; tests for accountability of, 8; tests for

validity of, 7–8. *See also* Bad advice; Effective advice; Inconsistent advice; Professional advice; Unactionable advice
Advocacy, purpose of, 76
Allaire, Paul, 45–46
Amalgamated Paper (AP), and structuring of strategic choices, 205–15
Ambiguity, 60–61
Anti-learning consequences, 60, 64–65
Appraisal: as basis for problem solving, 156–57; encouraging effective, 115
Assumptions, testing validity of, 103
Attributes, neither tested nor testable, 94–95
Attributions, untested, 226
Authenticity, 89; false roads to, 19–20

Bad advice, persistence of, 52–81
Bauman, R.P., 39
Behavior(s): causal factors of, 220–21; changing actual, 118–22